Bloom's
GUIDES

William Shakespeare's
Hamlet

1984
All the Pretty Horses
Beloved
Brave New World
Cry, the Beloved Country
Death of a Salesman
Hamlet
The Handmaid's Tale
The House on Mango Street
I Know Why the Caged Bird Sings
The Scarlet Letter
To Kill a Mockingbird

Bloom's
GUIDES

William Shakespeare's
Hamlet

Edited & with an Introduction
by Harold Bloom

CHELSEA HOUSE
PUBLISHERS
An imprint of Infobase Publishing

Bloom's Guides: Hamlet

Chelsea House
An imprint of Infobase Publishing
132 West 31st Street
New York NY 10001

Library of Congress Cataloging-in-Publication Data
Applied for.
ISBN: 0-7910-7571-0

Chelsea House books are available at special discounts when purchased in bulk quantities for businesses, associations, institutions, or sales promotions. Please call our Special Sales Department in New York at (212) 967-8800 or (800) 322-8755.

You can find Chelsea House on the World Wide Web at
http://www.chelseahouse.com

Contributing editor: Janyce Marson
Cover design by Takeshi Takahashi

Printed in the United States of America

Bang EJB 10 9 8 7 6 5 4 3 2 1

This book is printed on acid-free paper.

Contents

Introduction

HAROLD BLOOM

The largest mistake we can make about the play, *Hamlet*, is to think that it is the tragedy of a man who could not make up his mind, because (presumably) he thinks too much. Though Shakespeare adopts the subgenre of revenge tragedy, his drama has only superficial resemblances to other Elizabethan and Jacobean visions of revenge. The fundamental fact about Hamlet is not that he thinks too much, but that he thinks much too well. His is simply the most intelligent role ever written for the Western stage; indeed, he may be the most intelligent figure in all of world literature, West or East. Unable to rest in illusions of any kind, he thinks his way through to the truth, which may be a pure nihilism, yet a nihilism so purified that it possesses an absolute nobility, even a kind of transcendentalism. At the close Hamlet reasons that, since none of us knows anything about anyone else he leaves behind, what does it matter whether we leave at one time or another? Therefore let it be: the readiness or willingness to depart for that undiscovered country, death, from which no traveler returns, is for the matured Hamlet all in all. The rest is silence.

Shakespeare's longest and most notorious drama, *Hamlet* has imbued four centuries of interpreters with an endless capacity for wonder. We can be spurred to perpetually fresh surmises each time Hamlet speaks, because of a singular element in his consciousness. No other figure in the world's literature seems so much an authorial consciousness in his own right, as though he himself were composing Shakespeare's tragedy. The play itself tells us that he composes a small but significant part of it, by revising *The Murder of Gonzago* (a nonexistent work) into *The Mousetrap*, in order to catch the conscience of the murderous usurper, King Claudius. We do not know exactly which are Hamlet's contributions, but I must think that they include the great speech of the Player-King that concludes:

Our wills and fates do so contrary run
That our devices still are overthrown,
Our thoughts are ours, their ends none of our own.

Freud thought that there were no accidents, so that there was sense in everything, our characters being one with our fates. Hamlet teaches us otherwise, when his Player-King says: "Purpose is but the slave to memory." We find Hamlet's bleak wisdom difficult to absorb, if only because Hamlet is so charismatic a personality, as much so as King David in 2 Samuel or any other secular figure. I use "charismatic" in the sociologist Max Weber's sense: charisma is something that comes from outside the natural sphere, analogous to divine grace, though a displacement of it. Hamlet has an aura about him that never abandons him, even when his feigned madness crosses the line into serious disorder. Shakespeare has a handful of roles almost as intelligent as Hamlet's: Falstaff in the *Henry IV* plays, Portia in *The Merchant of Venice*, Rosalind in *As You Like It*, Cleopatra, and the great villains Iago in *Othello* and Edmund in *King Lear*. But not even Falstaff and Cleopatra have a charisma comparable to Hamlet's. He is beyond us; G. Wilson Knight suggested that Hamlet was death's ambassador to us. Perhaps he is; in Act V, Hamlet speaks with the authority of that undiscovered country, and he hints that he could tell us something crucial if only he had time enough. Death does not permit it, but we receive a hint that the hero's final awareness of eternity is centered in his relation to us, in his concern not to leave a wounded name behind him.

Nietzsche, in the spirit of Hamlet, observed that we only can find words for that which is already dead in our hearts, so that there always is a kind of contempt in the act of speaking. But that is the earlier Hamlet, who seems at least a decade younger than the disinterested sage who returns from the sea to endure the catastrophe of the play's final act. The matured Hamlet who speaks to Horatio has no contempt for expression when he says; "Thou wouldst not think how ill all's here about my heart—." There no longer is a kind of fighting in his heart; the civil war within him has been replaced by intimations of the end. If, as Horatio elegizes, a noble heart cracks with Hamlet's death, we can interpret "noble" in its original sense of "seeing." A seeing heart is Hamlet's final identity, which is very different from the grief-filled, almost traumatized prince whom we encounter as the play opens. Shakespeare, the greatest master of representing changes in the soul, created the most mutable of all his protagonists in Hamlet. Each time that he overhears himself, Hamlet changes, and his radical inwardness continues to augment. Insofar as the history of Western consciousness features a perpetually growing inward self, Hamlet is the central hero of that consciousness.

Some critics have felt that Hamlet is too large a figure even for his own play; that seems to be the true basis for T. S. Eliot's peculiar judgment that his drama was "an aesthetic failure." What, one wonders, is an aesthetic success if *Hamlet* is a failure? And yet, Hamlet does walk out of his play, much as Sir John Falstaff seems to stride out of the two parts of *Henry IV*. Like the Don Quixote and Sancho Panza of Cervantes, Hamlet and Falstaff are universal creations, who stimulate us to envision them in situations and in enterprises not necessarily present in the original texts. Still, the qualities that elevate these four above other literary characters *are* very much present upon the page. In Hamlet's case, it is manifest that revenge is hardly a suitable quest for his greatness, even if revenge were morally less equivocal than it actually is. For so large and exalted a consciousness, one wants a quest comparable in scope to that of Dante the Pilgrim in *The Divine Comedy*. Hamlet palpably is aware of the disproportion between his spirit and the project of revenge; the enigma is why Shakespeare designed his most capacious role as the centerpiece in a domestic tragedy of blood.

A multitude of readers and playgoers, rightly or wrongly, have felt that there must be a very personal relationship between Hamlet and Shakespeare. We know that Shakespeare himself acted the part of the ghost of Hamlet's father when the play was first staged. To think of Hamlet as Shakespeare's son is a very fanciful notion, brilliantly worked out by James Joyce's Stephen Dedalus in the Library scene of *Ulysses*. Shakespeare's only son, Hamnet, whose name differs from Hamlet's by only a single letter, died in 1596 at the age of eleven, less than five years before the play was written. What seems more apposite is A. C. Bradley's observation that Hamlet is the only Shakespearean character who seems capable of writing the play in which he appears. It would be extraordinary if Shakespeare, who imagined Hamlet, had possessed aspects of consciousness left unexplored in Hamlet. Sometimes I entertain another fancy, which is that Hamlet, who uncovers elements of reality that we would not have found for ourselves without him, performed something of the same function for Shakespeare himself.

Biographical Sketch

Few events in the life of William Shakespeare are supported by reliable evidence, and many incidents recorded by commentators of the last four centuries are either conjectural or apocryphal.

William Shakespeare was born in Stratford-upon-Avon on April 22 or 23, 1564, the son of Mary Arden and John Shakespeare, a tradesman. His early education was in the hands of a tutor, for his parents were probably illiterate. At age seven he entered the Free School in Stratford, where he learned the "small Latin and less Greek" attributed to him by Ben Jonson. When not in school Shakespeare may have gone to the popular Stratford fairs and to the dramas and mystery plays performed by traveling actors.

When Shakespeare was about thirteen his father removed him from school and apprenticed him to a butcher, although it is not known how long he remained in this occupation. When he was eighteen he married Anne Hathaway; their first child, Susanna, was born six months later. Twins Hamnet and Judith were born in February 1585. About this time Shakespeare was caught poaching deer on the estate of Sir Thomas Lucy of Cherlecot; Lucy's prosecution is said to have inspired Shakespeare to write his earliest literary work, a satire on his opponent. Shakespeare was convicted of poaching and forced to leave Stratford. He withdrew to London, leaving his family behind. He soon attached himself to the stage, initially in a menial capacity (as tender of playgoers' horses, according to one tradition), then as prompter's attendant. When the poaching furor subsided, Shakespeare returned to Stratford to join one of the many bands of itinerant actors. In the next five years he gained what little theatre training he received.

By 1592 Shakespeare was a recognized actor, and in that year he wrote and produced his first play, *Henry the Sixth, Part One*. Its success impelled Shakespeare soon afterward to write the second and third parts of *Henry the Sixth*. Shakespeare's popularity provoked the jealousy of Robert Greene, as recorded in his posthumous *Groats-worth of Wit* (1592). Shakespeare published *Venus and Adonis* in 1593, a poem based upon Ovid (or perhaps upon Arthur Golding's translation of Ovid's *Metamorphoses*). It was dedicated to the young Earl of Southampton—but perhaps without permission, a possible indication that Shakespeare was trying to gain the nobleman's patronage. However, the dedicatory address to Southampton in the poem *The Rape of Lucrece* (1594) reveals Shakespeare to have been on good terms with him. Many plays—such as *Titus Andronicus, The Comedy of Errors,* and *Romeo and Juliet*—were produced over the next several years, most performed by Shakespeare's troupe, the Lord Chamberlain's Company. In December 1594 Shakespeare acted in a comedy (of unknown authorship) before Queen Elizabeth; many other royal performances followed in the next decade.

In August 1596 Shakespeare's son Hamnet died. Early the next year Shakespeare bought a home, New Place, in the center of Stratford; he is said to have planted a mulberry tree in the back yard with his own hands. Shakespeare's relative prosperity is indicated by his purchasing more than a hundred acres of farmland in 1602, a cottage near his estate later that year, and half-interest in the tithes of some local villages in 1605.

In September 1598 Shakespeare began his friendship with the then unknown Ben Jonson by producing his play *Every Man in His Humour.* The next year the publisher William Jaggard affixed Shakespeare's name, without his permission, to a curious medley of poems under the title *The Passionate Pilgrim*; the majority of the poems were not by Shakespeare. Two of his sonnets, however, appeared in this collection, although the 154 sonnets, with their mysterious dedication to "Mr. W. H.," were not published as a group until 1609. Also in 1599 the Globe Theatre was built in Southwark (an area of London), and Shakespeare's company began acting there. Many of his greatest plays—*Troilus and Cressida, King Lear, Othello, Macbeth*—were performed in the Globe before its destruction by fire in 1613.

The death in 1603 of Queen Elizabeth, the last of the Tudors, and the accession of James I, from the Stuart dynasty of Scotland, created anxiety throughout England. Shakespeare's fortunes, however, were unaffected, as the new monarch extended the license of Shakespeare's company to perform at the Globe. James I saw a performance of Othello at the court in November 1604. In October 1605 Shakespeare's company performed before the Mayor and Corporation of Oxford. The last five years of Shakespeare's life seem void of incident; he had retired from the stage by 1613. Among the few known incidents is Shakespeare's involvement in a heated and lengthy dispute about the enclosure of common-fields around Stratford. He died on April 23, 1616, and was buried in the Church of St. Mary's in Stratford. A monument was later erected to him in the Poets' Corner of Westminster Abbey.

The Story Behind the Story

Theater

The period from 1599 to 1601 has been characterized as the Poets' War since the nineteenth century when Victorian scholars acknowledged that a quarrel between competing playwrights was embedded in a series of self-referential plays connected to each other through patterns of allusion and satire. In the mid-twentieth century, Alfred Harbage referred to this literary battle as the "War of the Theaters" in which the combatants were the rival repertory companies. Most recently, Renaissance scholars have granted the Poets' War the status it fully deserves as a controversy debating important theoretical and institutional issues within the context of the very competitive culture of late Elizabethan commercial theatre. The crux of that debate was the issue of dramatic representation. The battle lines were drawn in 1599 when Ben Jonson, who wanted to claim exclusive ownership of a persuasive form of dramatic representation, presented himself as Shakespeare's rival by inventing a new genre which he called "comical satire." Though Shakespeare responded to Jonson's attacks in a series of own satirical plays, *As You Like It*, *Twelfth Night* and *Troilus and Cressida*, the far more important consequence of this war between rival poets has been identified namely, that Shakespeare developed his own form of literary representation in the process.[1]

More specifically, with respect to *Hamlet*, the Poet's War is the critical context for understanding the "little eyases that cry out on the top of a question" ("a nest of young hawks") passage in Act II, scene ii. Rosencrantz here is referring to Ben Jonson's child actors, the Children of the Chapel, who have sullied the reputation of the adult actors, the "tragedians of the city," implying that they have slandered the Chamberlain Men performing at Shakespeare's Globe theatre. "These are now the fashion, and so berattle the common stages (so they call them) that many wearing rapiers are afraid of goose quills and dare scare come thither." Shakespeare is, of course, commenting on the controversy between the two types of commercial theatres, the public theatre of the Globe and the private theatres. Furthermore, Shakespeare is also accusing Jonson of exploiting these children who are made to ridicule the acting profession in general when they must "exclaim against their own succession" on stage, thereby destroying their future employment as adult performers. Indeed, Hamlet wonders how they are provided for, how they are "escoted." While a great deal more can be said of the Poets' War, and the relevant political and cultural conditions, what is perhaps most striking, as Critic James Bednarz points out, is that the most bitter indictments against the common stage came from within the theatre world itself, rather than the Puritans or any local authorities as might otherwise be assumed. But above all other considerations, Shakespeare's unique contribution to this controversy was his understanding that theatricality is inherent within us all. He "defended the common stages not by emphasizing the didactic power of poetry to transform its audience or the status of its performers, but by insisting that theatricality was the fundamental condition of human experience."[2]

Theatricality

In his discussion of theatricality in *Hamlet*, Richard Lanham identifies two parallel plots that work at cross-purposes with each other. The first plot, which he identifies as belonging to the hero Laertes, is a conventional revenge tragedy and is to be taken seriously in that the hero is, for the most part, straightforward in both his statements and his actions. The second and more compelling plot belongs to Hamlet, a very unconventional hero whose eloquence and endless deliberation on why he cannot consummate the revenge his father desires underscores his essential rhetorical role in the play. While Hamlet so eloquently describes his feelings, the question remains as to whether he actually feels them. *Hamlet* is a play in which "[e]veryone is manipulating everyone else with speechifying and then admitting he has done so." [3] Not only do these two "superposed plays" run counter to each other, they also create dual roles and opposing rhetorical significance for the other characters. Lanham reads *Hamlet* as a play in which all the characters are motivated by a desire for rhetorical demonstration because of their need for, and lack of, a dramatic equivalent for their feelings and their actions. This is certainly true for Hamlet, a consummate rhetorician who consistently makes misleading statements, revels in punning and double entendres while rendering searing indictments of all others. A similar statement could be made for Polonius who equally enjoys rhetorical gamesmanship. With a propensity for equivocation, Polonius appears to be an adept rhetorician, but is no match for Hamlet's intellect and command of language. A quasi-allegorical incarnation of the evils of rhetoric, Polonius lacks good judgment and insight. With an unwavering desire for eavesdropping on Hamlet while hiding behind a tapestry, Polonius's predilection for deception ultimately causes him to become the agent of his own demise.

Most recently, Harold Bloom has taken the counter-revenge theme further, stating that "Hamlet is part of Shakespeare's revenge upon revenge tragedy, and is of no genre. Of all poems, it is the most unlimited. As a meditation upon human fragility in confrontation with death, it competes only with the world's scriptures."[4] In *Hamlet: Poem Unlimited*, Bloom presents a reading which demonstrates the pervasiveness of theatricality within the character of Hamlet and the play which bears his name. Theatricality becomes the story beneath the story of the preternatural Prince who seemingly is preoccupied with exposing Claudius's murderous crime yet remains unable to avenge his father's death. However, viewed from the perspective of Hamlet as a playwright and stage manager, concerned with such contemporary issues as the status of acting companies and the works of his contemporaries, the traditional critical question of why he delays in consummating his father's revenge is answered by the recognition of a hidden agenda. Bloom describes Hamlet as "a kind of changeling, nurtured by Yorick, yet fathered by himself, an actor-playwright from the start," and an intellectual possessing a consciousness beyond comparison. Hamlet is seen as a character whose greatness is incommensurate with the calamitous state of affairs in

Denmark. Indeed, outside a theatrical context, Hamlet's story is really quite bizarre and inexplicable. Theatricality extends from the second scene of Act I when Hamlet delivers a searing indictment of Claudius and Gertrude through the end of Act V as he stages and authorizes his own death. The inclusion of plays within plays in *Hamlet*, which are performed for reasons beyond the desire to expose Claudius's guilt, provides a platform from which Hamlet can direct the company of actors and subvert all conventional notions of revenge tragedy. For Bloom, theatricality also extends to the other characters: the omnipresent Horatio serves as Hamlet's "perpetual audience"; Claudius is "a minor league rhetorician" and "a puny opposite for the Prince"; and Laertes, whose "fustian rhetoric" pales in comparison to Hamlet's "scandalous eloquence."

Tired of playacting, Hamlet's theatrical nature comes to an end as he becomes concerned only with a wounded name and delivers his final instructions to Horatio. With a consciousness too large for the play in which he has been confined, the Prince is ready for a death which to him is an apotheosis. Indeed, as Bloom points out, Hamlet's final words, "let it be," are addressed directly to us, his audience, signaling that representation has been abandoned for the thing itself. Hamlet's death does not signal his embarkation to an imaginative other world but, rather, a release from the responsibility of "an ever-burgeoning self-consciousness."

Notes

1. James A. Bednarz. "Ben John and the 'Little Eyases': Theatrical Politics in *Hamlet*." In his *Shakespeare & the Poets' War*. New York: Columbia University Press (2001): 225–56.

2. *Ibid*, 253.

3. Richard Lanham. "Superposed Plays: *Hamlet*." In his *The Motives of Eloquence: Literary Rhetoric in the Renaissance*. New Haven and London: Yale University Press (1976): 129–43.

4. Harold Bloom. "Inferring Hamlet." In his '*Hamlet*': *Poem Unlimited*. New York: Riverhead Books (2003): 3.

List of Characters

Hamlet, prince of Denmark, is the principal character of the play. Though a speech by the gravedigger (5.1) pinpoints Hamlet's age at thirty, there is reason to believe that he may be younger: he is a student, and the peer of a generation (including Laertes and Fortinbras) that is only beginning to come into its own. Returning to Denmark to attend the funeral of his father the king and the remarriage of his mother to Claudius, Hamlet is visited by the ghost of his father. The ghost relates how he was murdered by Claudius, and commands Hamlet to seek revenge. Much of the play is spent exploring Hamlet's complicated frame of mind in the period of time between his promise to the ghost and his murder of Claudius in the play's final scene.

Old Hamlet is Hamlet's father, the former King of Denmark who was murdered by his brother, Claudius. His ghost haunts both the prince and the play, commanding Hamlet to avenge his murder. Old Hamlet was apparently a powerful warrior in his day, having both conquered Poland and besting the king of Norway in single combat. Old Hamlet occupies a special place in his son's imagination. Hamlet repeatedly describes him as an ideal of manhood, a representative of a heroic age that may be irretrievably lost.

Gertrude is Hamlet's mother, the widow of Old Hamlet, and the wife of Claudius. We know that she dotes upon her son, but we do not know how she feels about her first husband, her relation to her second husband's guilt, or her son's accusations. Though she herself is only sketchily presented, she plays a major role in Hamlet's inner struggle: on several occasions he bitterly complains of her failure to honor Old Hamlet's memory, and his ambivalence about her seems to color his response to Ophelia. Gertrude is accidentally killed at the end of the play, when she drinks poison intended for her son.

Claudius, Hamlet's uncle, becomes King of Denmark by killing his brother, old King Hamlet and marrying his widow, Gertrude. Though troubled by a guilty conscience and provoked to further villainy by Hamlet's erratic behavior, Claudius attempts throughout to maintain public order in Denmark. After plotting with Laertes to poison Hamlet during a fencing match, Claudius is killed by the poison intended for the prince.

Horatio is Hamlet's friend and confidant. Horatio, like Hamlet, has studied at Wittenburg: he is presented as learned and reliable, though lacking the prince's imagination. Horatio assists Hamlet throughout the play. As Hamlet dies, he makes Horatio promise to report the truth on all that has taken place.

Polonius is the father of Laertes and Ophelia, and adviser to Claudius. He is represented as a comically sententious, nosy old man, and as the dispenser of long-winded and clichéd advice. His nosiness proves to be his undoing: in service to the king, he hides behind a tapestry to eavesdrop when Hamlet visits his mother; Hamlet hears him, and stabs him to death. Polonius's death drives Ophelia mad, provokes in Laertes a murderous rage for vengeance, and convinces Claudius that Hamlet must be sent to England and quietly executed.

Ophelia is the sister of Laertes and daughter of Polonius. Though Hamlet has been courting her, Ophelia willingly obeys her father when he tells her to discourage the prince's advances. Later, she bears the brunt of Hamlet's acerbic cynicism on more than one occasion. When Polonius is killed, she is driven mad and accidentally drowns herself. Ophelia is presented throughout the play as loving, innocent, and obedient. Victimized by the play's tragic actions, her madness and subsequent death are rendered poignantly and are fully undeserved.

Laertes is the son of Polonius and brother of Ophelia. At the start of the play Laertes leaves for France, but returns in a rage at the news of his father's death. Laertes is presented throughout the play as Hamlet's peer, rival, and counterpart. His passionate desire to avenge his father's murder stands in marked contrast to Hamlet's inaction. In the carnage of the final scene, Laertes kills—and is in turn killed by—Hamlet.

Fortinbras is the son of the late king of Norway. He is also the leader of an army of "lawless resolutes" with which, as the play begins, he plans to recapture the lands that old Hamlet won from his father in single combat. The king of Norway forbids the attack, and Fortinbras leads his troops into Poland instead. Like Laertes, Fortinbras functions in the play as a foil for Hamlet, for his desire to attack Denmark is also an attempt to avenge his father's death at the hands of Old Hamlet. Fortinbras and his army enter the Danish court during the play's final scene, just as Hamlet, Laertes, Claudius, and Gertrude are dying. With the support of the dying prince, Fortinbras assumes the mantle of authority in Denmark.

Rosencrantz and Guildenstern are old friends of Hamlet's and would-be courtiers summoned by Claudius and Gertrude to discover the root of Hamlet's melancholy. Hamlet's treatment of them goes from friendly to scornful as it becomes increasingly clear that they are motivated only by their interest in the king's favor. Claudius sends them with Hamlet to England, and orders them to deliver his letters to the English king. These letters contain orders for Hamlet's execution, though it is not clear that Rosencrantz and Guildenstern know this. Hamlet steals the letters from them, and replaces them with a forged letter ordering their execution instead. As the play ends, ambassadors from England arrive with news that the pair has been killed.

Summary and Analysis

The *Tragedy of Hamlet, Prince of Denmark* opens on a dark and foreboding scene where nervous sentinels cross paths during their nightly watch. And, among this group of guards is Hamlet's friend and confidante, Horatio. We soon learn the reason for their anxiety, namely that during the past two nights they have been visited by a ghostly apparition in the form of Old Hamlet—the recently deceased father of the prince that bears his name. Horatio, a scholar like Prince Hamlet, is at first skeptical that the ghost will reappear, believing it to be a figment of the guards' imagination; but when it does, Horatio exclaims that he is filled with "fear and wonder." Nevertheless, the ghost of the old King crosses the stage quickly, ignoring Horatio's rude attempts to speak with it. "What art thou that usurp'st this time of night ... By heaven, I charge thee, speak."

Horatio also provides historical and political context when he interprets the apparition as an omen signaling a pending catastrophe for Denmark, for it is endangered by the prospect of an attack by an army of Norwegian brigands under the command of young Fortinbras. In the years preceding the time of *Hamlet*, the former king Hamlet had killed Fortinbras's father (who was then king of Norway) in single combat, and by doing so won possession of Norwegian lands. The young Fortinbras is now preparing an army to reconquer the territory his father lost. As Horatio and the guards are discussing the possible link between the threat of war and the appearance of the ghost, the latter reappears. Again Horatio attempts to speak with it, at first deferentially, offering to assist it with good deeds, but becomes increasingly desperate, to the point that Marcellus is ordered to stop it by force, and once again offends this otherworldly spirit. "We do it wrong, being so majestical, / To offer it the show of violence," explains Marcellus. However, it is soon observed that the rooster's crow has just sounded, announcing the coming of day, at which time "no spirit dare stir abroad." It is decided that young Hamlet should accompany the watch on the following evening.

From this opening scene of darkness and strange visitations, we now enter a scene of ceremony and celebration at the Danish court **(Act 1, scene 2).** Nevertheless, despite the abrupt change in scene where the formality of courtly language and the pretense of an orderly state emits an aura of confidence, the audience cannot so easily forget the terrors of the nightwatch. As the scene opens, Claudius (brother of the recently-deceased King Hamlet) is performing the public offices of kingship. Though he acknowledges a communal grief at the passing of Old Hamlet, declaring the "whole kingdom / To be contracted in one brow of woe," and gracefully alludes to his own marriage to Old Hamlet's widow, Gertrude, "our sometime sister, now our queen, / Th' imperial jointress to this warlike state," there is something very insincere, even shocking, in his speech. For Claudius has just married Gertrude on the heels of Old Hamlet's demise, glibly acknowledging the rapid course of events, "with mirth in funeral, and with dirge in marriage, / In equal scale weighing delight and dole." Claudius continues by thanking everyone for their support, dispatches his ambassadors to Fortinbras's uncle, the current king of Norway, asking him to stop his nephew's warlike ambitions and, finally, grants young Laertes leave to travel to France.

Having performed his state functions, Claudius turns his attention to Hamlet, who has recently returned from his studies in Wittenburg in order to attend the funeral of his father and the wedding of his newly widowed mother to Claudius. From the very beginning, Hamlet becomes the focal point of attention at court. Dressed in funeral attire, he is the sole figure on the crowded stage dressed in the "customary suits of solemn black," and his manner of speaking is in sharp contrast to the formal rhetoric of state functions, for Hamlet's responses are full of puns, double entendres, and bitterness towards the outrageous pretenses of Claudius and Gertrude. Interestingly, it is also here that Hamlet offers a clue to his true theatrical genius he will display throughout the course of the play when he tells Gertrude that his melancholic demeanor reveals only a small part of his true feelings. "These indeed seem, / For they are actions that a man might play, / But I have that within which passes show— / These but the trappings and the suits of woe." Claudius and Gertrude both ask Hamlet to remain in Denmark, and he agrees. The court then departs, leaving Hamlet alone on stage, and he delivers the first of his famous soliloquies, or dramatic monologues, that punctuate the play. "O, that this too too sallied flesh would melt, / Thaw, and resolve itself into a dew."

These soliloquies are of great importance as they provide a glimpse into Hamlet's private thoughts, which are continually weighed against his public statements and actions. In this first soliloquy, we learn that Hamlet has an exalted opinion of his father, "So excellent a king, that was to this / Hyperion to a satyr, so loving to my mother," and a revulsion towards women stemming from his disgust at Gertrude's quick and incestuous remarriage to her brother-in-law Claudius. "Frailty, thy name is woman." Horatio appears on the heels of Hamlet's soliloquy with news of the ghost, and Hamlet agrees to join the watch at the appointed time.

In **Act 1, scene 3,** the scene shifts to young Laertes as he is preparing to depart for France. Here, he offers advice to his sister, Ophelia, cautioning her about Hamlet's overtures of love to her. Though we already sense that Hamlet is very much his own person, willing to defy all conventional and political expectations, Laertes is keenly aware of Hamlet's royal status and reminds Ophelia of the dual nature of kingship. "He may not, as unvalued persons do, / Carve for himself, for on his choice depends / The safety and health of this whole state." When their father, Polonius, enters, he cautions his daughter about guarding her chastity and orders her to cut off all communication with the prince.

As **scene 4** begins Hamlet and Horatio join the sentinels in their watch at night, while a boisterous party at court is heard in the background. To Hamlet's great astonishment, the ghost soon reappears and beckons to him. Though the others try to dissuade him, Hamlet believes he must follow the ghost regardless of any danger and even threatens to kill anyone who tries to prevent him. Alone with Prince Hamlet (**scene 5**), the apparition announces that he is in fact the spirit of Old Hamlet, "doomed for a certain term to walk the night," and promises a story "whose lightest word / Would harrow up the soul, freeze thy young blood." The ghost tells Hamlet how his brother Claudius murdered him by pouring poison in his ear while he slept, and then seduced his wife. "Thus was I sleeping by a brother's hand / Of life, of crown, of queen at once dispatched." Moreover, since old Hamlet was murdered while sleeping, he never had a chance to receive absolution for his earthly sins and has suffered terrible torments in purgatory. "Cut off even in the blossoms of my sin, / Unhousel'd, disappointed, unanel'd." Old Hamlet then gives his son specific commands to avenge his murder by killing Claudius, but not harm his mother, Gertrude. The Ghost then departs, calling "adieu, adieu, adieu. Remember me." Hamlet's response to the ghost's poignant departure, confirms his belief that his mother's overhasty marriage was terribly wrong and that Claudius is despicable and evil. Furthermore, his meeting with the ghost seemingly makes Hamlet resolute in accomplishing the revenge his father so richly desires. "And thy commandment all alone shall live / Within the book and volume of my brain." Rejoined by Horatio and a guard, Hamlet greets them, but refuses to tell them what has transpired. Hamlet asks his companions three times to swear absolute secrecy about what they have seen; each time the voice of the ghost echoes "swear" from below the stage, and each time, they swear to keep silent. Interestingly, in yet another suggestion about the theatricality of his personality, Hamlet intimates that it may be necessary for him to "put an antic disposition on"— and requests that his companions understand and maintain absolute secrecy about any strange behavior he may display in the future.

Act 2, scene 1 opens with Ophelia reporting to her father that she has seen Hamlet, and that he is in physical and emotional disarray. "Lord Hamlet with his doublet all unbraced, / No hat upon his head, his stockings fouled, / ... As if had been looséd out of hell." To which strange appearance Polonius erroneously attributes to overwhelming love, as the transport of someone to an unearthly realm. "This is the very ecstasy of love / Whose violent property fordoes itself." Polonius resolves to speak to the King straight away.

As **scene 2** opens, the King and Queen have commissioned Rosencrantz and Guildenstern to discover the cause of Hamlet's inexplicable behavior, which Claudius describes as Hamlet's transformation, "Sith nor th'exterior nor the inward man / Resembles that it was." As they embark on the King's commission, Polonius once again protests that he has discovered the true cause of Hamlet's "lunacy," and immediately thereafter goes off to greet Voltemand and Cornelius to learn the news from Norway. While Claudius wants to believe Polonius's diagnosis, Gertrude is able to articulate the truth, attributing Hamlet's behavior to "[h]is father's death and our o'erhasty marriage." But Polonius soon returns and reads a letter from Hamlet to Ophelia in order to prove his theory that Hamlet is mad "with hot love on the wing."

At Polonius suggestion, the King and Queen agree to hide behind an arras, in order to observe Hamlet's behavior towards Ophelia. Hamlet first enters, reading a book and appearing completely mad, correctly labeling Polonius "a fishmongerer" and advising him: "for yourself, sir, shall grow old as I am, if like a crab you could go backward." In an aside, Polonius admits to himself that this display of madness notwithstanding, Hamlet may in fact be in control. Polonius recognizes a "method" to Hamlet's "madness" and that madness indeed has a special access to truth: "How pregnant sometimes his replies are! a happiness that often madness hits on, which reason and sanity could not so prosperously be delivered of."

Rosencrantz and Guildenstern enter later in the same scene, at which time Hamlet begins an inquiry as to their true motive in visiting him. Through a series of probing questions and witty repartee, Hamlet accuses Fortune of being the "strumpet" who has sent these same two friends to prison, i.e. Denmark. And his distrust of women, which is increasing, is likewise equated with being in Denmark. "O God, I could be bounded in a nutshell and count myself a king of infinite space, were it not that I have bad dreams." When his two companions admit that they were sent to discover the cause of his insanity, Hamlet gives them a true description of his state of mind but does not outwardly appear to fully understand himself. "I have of late—but wherefore I know not—lost all mirth, forgone all custom of exercises; and indeed it goes so heavily with my disposition ... Man delights not me; no, nor woman neither...." However, Rosencrantz and Guildenstern have brought with them a company of players whom they passed on the way. And, no sooner does Hamlet greet these young players than we begin to see that Hamlet recognizes himself as a fellow actor.

Towards the end of the scene, Hamlet displays his full theatrical skills as a consummate playwright and director, instructing the players to perform *The Murder of Gonzago*, asking them to memorize some dozen or so lines of his own composition which he will insert into the play. As Rosencrantz and Guildenstern leave, Hamlet delivers another soliloquy, in which he begins with self-reproach "O, what a rogue and peasant slave I am? ... / Prompted to my revenge by heaven and hell, / Must like a whore unpack my heart with words." It is interesting to note a suggestion of Hamlet's theatricality here. An actor is "prompted" when he has forgotten his line. In fact, earlier in this same speech, Hamlet has described his father's command as his "cue" to action, implying that although Hamlet knows his filial duty, he feels more like an actor preparing for a role rather than a son. Towards the end of this soliloquy, Hamlet begins to suspect the ghost's veracity, because of the devil's protean abilities to assume "a pleasing shape" and decides to test the ghost's story by asking the players to enact a murder resembling Old Hamlet's in a play put on before the court. If Claudius responds with guilt, then the ghost's report is true. In any event, Hamlet concludes this speech with an absolute determination to prove Claudius's culpability. "The play's the thing / Wherein I'll catch the conscience of the King."

At the beginning of **Act 3 (scene 1)**, Claudius is questioning Rosencrantz and Guildenstern as to whether they have discovered the cause of Hamlet's "turbulence and dangerous lunacy." They respond that Hamlet professes himself to be "distracted." Yet, a serious question arises as to whether Prince Hamlet may in fact be manipulating everyone else into believing him insane. Guildenstern echoes Polonius's previous observation that there is a method to this madness, implying once again that Hamlet may very well be in full control of his emotions. "Nor do we find him forward to be sounded / But with a crafty madness keeps aloof." In the meantime, Polonius suggests, and Claudius agrees, that the two should hide and observe Hamlet and Ophelia, to determine whether it be "the affliction of love or no."

When Hamlet enters, delivering his most poignant soliloquy, he reveals an inner torment and struggle with his inability to avenge his father's murder. "To be or not to be, that is the question: / Whether 'tis nobler in the mind to suffer / The slings and arrows of outrageous fortune, / Or to take arms against a sea of troubles, / And by opposing end them." At the end of this soliloquy as he meets with Ophelia, Hamlet's anger against women resurfaces. He states that although he did love her once because of her beauty, he now believes that same beauty to be another aspect of dissembling womanhood and wants to banish her from his thoughts. "Get thee to a nunnery. Why wouldst thou be a breeder of sinners?" An astounded Ophelia responds, "O, what a noble mind is here o'erthrown!" Immediately following this declaration, King Claudius enters, with Polonius, stating that Hamlet's condition is not that of love, and demanding that he be sent speedily to England to avoid his danger to the state. "Madness in great ones must not unwatched go."

Hamlet is speaking to the actors as **scene 2** opens, giving them very specific stage directions. He appears to be very rational, and resolute, and in full control of his faculties. "Speak the speech, I pray you, as I pronounced it to you, trippingly on the tongue, ... Be not too tame neither, but let your own discretion by your tutor.... hold as 'twere the mirror up to nature." As further affirmation of his self-command, Hamlet responds to his earlier quandary. "Give me that man / That is not passion's slave, and I will wear him / In my heart's core, ay, in my heart of heart."

Following the successful performance of the modified play—and after the startled Claudius abruptly ends the entertainment—Hamlet discusses Claudius's distress with Rosencrantz and Guildenstern. Hamlet shrewdly states that he cannot help the King, "for me to put him to his purgation would perhaps plunge him into more choler." But his companions cannot understand this puzzlingly response because they do not truly understand Hamlet's dissembling nature. "Good my lord, put your discourse into some frame, and start not so wildly from my affair." Indeed, Hamlet is in complete control playing on the emotions of his interlocutors. To Rosencrantz his response is that he cannot "[m]ake you a wholesome answer; my wit's diseased" and to Guildenstern, whom he has just challenged by presenting him with a recorder to play on, he declares that he cannot be manipulated: "[c]all me what instrument you will, though you can fret me, you cannot play upon me." As scene 2 concludes, Hamlet is now alone and preparing to speak with his mother. In this he will do the Ghost's bidding, careful not to cause her physical harm. "Let me be cruel, not unnatural; / I will speak daggers to her, but use none. / My tongue and soul in this be hypocrites."

In **scene 3**, Claudius's distress increases as he tells Rosencrantz and Guildenstern that Prince Hamlet is a dangerous madman who threatens the state and must therefore be exiled. "I like him not, nor stands it safe with us / To let his madness range.... I your commission will forthwith dispatch, / And he to England shall along with you." Promising their obedience to the King's command, Rosencrantz muses of the dual nature of the kingship—the king's mortal existence and the burden he must bear in his manifestation of the body politic. "It is a massy wheel / ... To whose huge spokes then thousand lesser things / Are mortised and adjoined."

In **scene 4**, as Hamlet is on his way to speak with the Queen, his thoughts return to his father and he again debates with himself about the appropriate time and circumstances to perform the long-awaited revenge upon the now-terrified

Claudius. "Up, sword, and know thou a more horrid hent. / When he is drunk asleep, or in his rage, / Or in th' incestuous pleasure of his bed, / ... That has no relish of salvation in't—." When Hamlet finally confronts his mother, he forces her to look at herself in a mirror, "[w]here you may see the inmost part of you." Hamlet then hears a noise behind the arras (curtain) and stabs the eavesdropping Polonius to death with his sword. Ignoring the fallen Polonius, Hamlet quickly returns to the purpose of showing his mother the full extent of her sins. While he declares Claudius to be "[a] king of shreds and patches," the Ghost enters, invisible to Gertrude who believes Hamlet to be completely mad. "Alas, how is't with you, / That you do bend your eye on vacancy, / And with th'incorporal air do hold discourse? Forth at your eyes your spirits wildly peep, / ... Your bedded hair like life in excrements / Start up and stand an end. / ... Whereon do you look?" Hamlet responds that he is perfectly rational and in control and, further, challenges the Queen to test that rationality. "It is not madness / That I have uttered. Bring me to the test, / And I the matter will re-word, which madness / Would gambol from." Dragging Polonius's body into an adjoining room, Hamlet calmly bids his mother goodnight and declares that he must now depart for England.

Act 4 (scene 1) begins with a very distressed Gertrude telling Claudius of the noble Polonius's murder by a deranged Hamlet. "Mad as the sea and wind when both contend / ... And in this brainish apprehension kills / The unseen good old man." To which Claudius responds that Hamlet's "liberty is full of threats to all." The king immediately sends Rosencrantz and Guildenstern after Hamlet, hoping that they will be able at least to find the old man's body. They come upon Hamlet just as he has "stowed" the corpse **(scene 2)** and Hamlet is openly scornful of their attempts to question him. When asked what he has done with the dead body, Hamlet responds that he has "compounded it with dust, whereto 'tis kin."

However, as Claudius observes in **scene 3**, Hamlet is beloved by his subjects and cannot be so easily defeated. "How dangerous is it that this man goes loose! / Yet must we not put the strong law on him. / He's loved of the distracted multitude." When Claudius questions Hamlet as to the whereabouts of Polonius, Hamlet, in full command of his incisive wit, muses on the universality of death and responds that the old fishmongerer has been justly disposed of. "Not where he eats, but where he is eaten. / A certain convocation of politic worms are e'en at him." The king hurriedly dispatches Hamlet (along with Rosencrantz and Guildenstern) to England, along with letters addressed to the English king ordering Hamlet's execution. "Do it, England, / For like the hectic in my blood he rages, / And thou must cure me."

Scene 4 finds Hamlet and his escorts heading toward the coast, where they encounter Fortinbras and his army. By talking to a captain, Hamlet discovers that the army is marching toward Poland, impelled by honor to do battle over a worthless plot of ground, "that hath in it no profit but the name." Hamlet reflects that this waste of life is a social disease, th' imposthume of much wealth and peace, / That inward breaks, and shows no cause without / Why the man dies." Telling his escorts to go ahead, Hamlet delivers his fourth and final soliloquy, in which he debates the cause and consequences of his delay in achieving the revenge upon Claudius. "How all occasions do inform against me, / And spurt my dull revenge! ... Rightly to be great / Is not to stir without great argument, / But greatly to find a quarrel in a straw / When honor's at the stake." Concluding that greatness lies in the capacity to care, he rededicates his commitment to avenge his father's murder. "O, from this time forth, / My thoughts be bloody, or be nothing worth!"

Scene 5 shows the tragic consequences of Polonius's death for his daughter and son. As Ophelia goes mad with grief, her madness takes the form of an extreme and touching flightiness expressed in incomplete sentences. "Her speech is nothing. / Yet the unshaped use of it doth move / The hearers to collection; they aim at it, And botch the words up fit to their own thoughts." She wanders in and out of the scene singing snatches of ballads and speaking in poignantly nonsensical fragments. Meanwhile, Laertes returns from France, "in a riotous head," gathers a mob of supporters who declare him their leader, "choose we, Laertes shall be king," and when he learns of Polonius's death from Claudius, and threatens to stop at nothing to avenge it. "To hell allegiance, vows to the blackest devil, / Conscience and grace to the profoundest pit! / I dare damnation." But Claudius is able to calm him somewhat by promising to help him get to the bottom of Polonius's death. "And where the great offence is, let the great axe fall." It is important to note here that Laertes's determination to redress the wrong done to his father is precisely what Hamlet has been hitherto unable to accomplish and his angry statements provide a deliberate contrast between the two characters. Furthermore, even Fortinbras demonstrates a determination to act though his plans are eventually thwarted. It is Hamlet alone who is unable to act.

At this point **(scene 6)** a sailor arrives, bearing a letter from Hamlet to Horatio. It seems that the ship bound for England has been attacked by pirates, and that only Hamlet was captured. In return for some undisclosed promise of service or otherwise, the pirates have left Hamlet on his native soil. Hamlet's letter also alludes to some secrets (presumably Claudius's villainy), and bids Horatio come to him at once. "I have words to speak in thine ear will make thee dumb."

In speaking with Laertes **(scene 7)**, Claudius discloses that Hamlet has murdered his father Polonius, to which Laertes responds by questioning the King's lack of response to these criminal acts. Claudius reminds Laertes that he could not take action against the young prince who is beloved by Gertrude and whose spellbinding charm has won the hearts of the people. "[T]he great love the general gender bear him; / Who dipping all his faults in their affection, / Work like the spring that turneth wood to stone." Nevertheless, Laertes wants to kill Hamlet at once, but Claudius gets him to agree to a craftier plan. In revealing to Laertes that Hamlet has been "envenomed with his envy" upon hearing a report on Laertes's prowess with swords, Claudius maintains that Hamlet would seize the chance to engage Laertes and that killing Hamlet in a duel would have the benefit of avoiding a public disturbance. "And for his death no wind of blame shall breathe." In such a match, Claudius suggests, it would be easy for Laertes to anoint his rapier with a deadly poison and adds that he will have a chalice full of poisoned wine ready to serve to the prince as a toast between rounds. That way, even if Laertes fails, Hamlet will die. Nevertheless, Claudius and, by extension, Laertes, miscalculate Hamlet's character, believing the Prince to be careless and incapable of planning a preconceived course of action. Claudius assures Laertes that "[h]e, being remiss, / Most generous and free from all contriving, / Will not peruse the foils." As they finalize these plans, Gertrude enters and reports that Ophelia has drowned, although no reason has been given.

Act 5, scene 1 begins in a graveyard, with the entry of two clowns who have come to prepare Ophelia's grave; they question whether she is to be given a Christian burial as the possibility of her death being a suicide is left open. Hamlet and Horatio enter as one of the clowns sings while he digs, unaware that the grave being readied is for Ophelia. Holding up one of the skulls strewn about the graveyard, Hamlet reflects on the equality of death, where all earthly distinctions of social class and individual achievement are obliterated, and in so doing, introduces a common theme found in Renaissance texts—the *memento mori*—reminders of death."Why may not that be the skull of a lawyer? Where be his quiddities now, his quillets, his cases, his tenures, and his tricks. Why does he suffer this mad knave now to knock him about the sconce with a dirty shovel, and will not tell him of his action of battery?" And among the skulls, Hamlet finds that of Yorick, the court jester and Prince Hamlet's beloved childhood playmate. In one of Shakespeare's most poignant speeches, Hamlet tells Horatio of his love for Yorick. "A fellow of infinite jest, of most excellent fancy. He hath bore me on his back a thousand times, and now how abhorred in my imagination it is!" But Hamlet's reverie is interrupted with the arrival of Ophelia's funeral party, and he is startled to discover that the grave he has been standing by is hers. Laertes laments wildly over his sister's body, leaps into her grave, and demands to be buried alongside her. "Hold off the earth awhile, / Till I have caught her once more in mine arms." But Laertes's passion serves to provoke Hamlet's anger to such an extent that the prince leaps into Ophelia's grave and attempts to outdo Laertes. Never to be bested in theatrical skills, Hamlet once again demonstrates that he is in complete control from start to finish in the play that bears his name. "Be buried quick with her, and so will I. / And if thou prate of mountains, let them throw / Millions of acres on us ... I'll rant as well as thou." Claudius barely keeps the situation under control, asking Horatio to look after his friend, and reminding Laertes to be patient.

In **scene 2**, as Hamlet tells Horatio of his experiences at sea, he celebrates his ability to outwit Claudius and thus save his own life, despite seemingly insurmountable circumstances. After stealing Claudius's letter to the King of England from Rosencrantz and Guildenstern, Hamlet replaces it with a forged letter, sealed with his father's signet, thereby ordering their immediate execution. "Being thus benetted round with villainies, / Or I could make a prologue to my brains, / They had begun the play." And lest we think he has regrets, Hamlet makes it perfectly clear that he harbors no anxiety about his actions. "Why, many, they did make love to this employment. / They are not near my conscience; their defeat / Does by their own insinuation grow." Following this revelation, a foppish young courtier named Osric enters to announce that the king has wagered on Hamlet in a fencing match with Laertes. Despite feelings of misgiving, Hamlet agrees to participate in the duel. As Hamlet and Laertes face each other, the prince apologizes and Laertes accepts the apology, but stiffly responds that honor must be satisfied. Though the match begins auspiciously for Hamlet who manages to strike Laertes twice, the scene rapidly devolves into a massacre. Gertrude accidentally drinks the poisoned wine over the protestations of her husband, while Laertes stabs Hamlet with the poison rapier. In a scuffle, the two men exchange rapiers, causing Hamlet to inadvertently poison Laertes by striking him. Gertrude dies, and Laertes, who knows that he and Prince Hamlet have both been poisoned, tells Hamlet of the King's plot. Hamlet stabs Claudius with the poisoned rapier and then forces him to drink the dregs of the poisoned wine. In so doing,

Hamlet finally consummates the long anticipated revenge. On his deathbed, Hamlet implores Horatio to report honestly all that has transpired and names Fortinbras the new king of Denmark. As Fortinbras arrives, an ambassador from England arrives to report the execution of Rosencrantz and Guildenstern. *Hamlet* concludes with Horatio promising to tell the tale of Hamlet "to th' yet unknowing world," while Fortinbras orders his soldiers to prepare a military funeral for Hamlet. In the end, Hamlet has authorized the official record of his life.

Critical Views

HARLEY GRANVILLE-BARKER
ON DRAMATIC EXPRESSION

Few things throw more light on the nature of Shakespeare's art than does the fact that his masterpiece—not his greatest piece of work, perhaps, but the one in which he attains to a freedom and fullness of dramatic impression unknown before—should be the recasting, in all probability, of a ready-made play. Hamlet himself, it may be said, the most life-like and 'original' of his creations, was a ready-made character too; the conventional Elizabethan 'melancholy man.' His achievement was in the reconciling of these seeming contradictions.

But he 'wanted art,' said Jonson; and Milton implied it; and Dryden, despite his admiration for him, felt bound to confess it. And if we mean, as Jonson and Dryden will have meant, a scheme of consistent principles and a studied method of expressing them, the Shakespeare of the greater plays lacks that most decidedly. There is an aspect of him which turns towards pure beauty of form, and the discipline and the limitations involved. It shows in the poems and in the earlier plays—in the exceptional homogeneity of *Richard II* and the graces of *A Midsummer Night's Dream*—and we may divine it in his instructed love for the music of his time. Had he begun by writing plays to please himself, it is possible that the lyric poet in him would have prevailed. We can imagine him in Lyly's place, with schoolboys for his actors, delicate, docile instruments, to be taught their parts line by line; the result an etherealised semi-classic drama, of which Jonson could have approved without cavil. But he found himself instead learning his playwright's trade amid the comradely give-and-take of the common theatre workshop; and the result was very different. Let us cheerfully admit that he 'wanted art'; he was the genius of the workshop.

What he learnt there was to think directly in terms of the medium in which he worked; in the movement of the scene, in the humanity of the actors and their acting. Heroic acting, as Shakespeare found it, left the actor's identity with the character still not quite complete. It was comparable to those Japanese puppet-shows, in which the puppet, life-size and gorgeous, is handled by its black-suited showman in full view of the audience, who take pleasure in the patent skill of the handling. Tamburlaine was very much such a puppet. Alleyne himself wore the finery and went through the motions; but Marlowe had made the character something rather to be exhibited than acted. The trick of speech by which Tamburlaine and Zenocrate—Barabas, Hieronimo, Alphonsus and the rest—so often address themselves by name has its significance.

But the instinct of the actor is to identify himself with the character he plays, and this instinct Shakespeare the actor would naturally encourage Shakespeare the dramatist to gratify. The progress here is rapid. Richard III is still somewhat the magnificent puppet, yet the effect already will be less that of Burbage exhibiting the character than of Richard himself 'showing off.' The gain is great. With the actors forgetting themselves in their characters the spectators the more easily forget their own world for the world of the play. The illusion so created, we should note, is lodged in the actors and characters alone. Shakespeare's theatre does not lend itself to the visual illusion, which, by the aid of realistic scenery and lighting, seems physically to isolate them in that other world. But he can, helped by the ubiquity of his platform stage, preserve the intimacy which this sacrifices. His aim is to keep the actor, now identified with the character, in as close a relation to the spectators—as that by which the Clown, in his own right, exercises sway over them. It is not merely or mainly by being funny that the Clown captures and holds his audience, but by personal appeal, the intimacy set up, the persuading them that what he has to say is his own concern—and theirs. It is with the comic and semi-comic characters—from Angelica and Shylock to Falstaff—that we are first brought into this fellowship; and whatever conventions Shakespeare may discard, it will not be the revealing soliloquy and aside. A large part of the technical achievement of Hamlet lies in the bringing home his intimate griefs so directly to us. In whatever actor's guise we see him he is Hamlet, yet the appeal is as genuine as if the man before us were making it in his own person. But the actor does not lose himself in the character he plays. On the contrary. He not only presents it under his own aspect, he lends it his own emotions too, and he must re-pass the thought of which it is built through the sieve of his own mind: He dissects it and then reconstructs it in terms of his own personality. He realises himself in Hamlet. And if he did not his performance would be lifeless. The thing is as true of a Falstaff. If the humour is no more a part of the actor than the padding is, our laughter will be empty.

Shakespeare learnt the secret of this intimate and fruitful collaboration in the workshop of the theatre. And it is the dramatist's master-secret. He has to learn, for his part, just what sort of material to give to the actors of his characters; the nature, the quality, also the effective quantity of it, neither more nor less. If it is dialogue of little more substance than have the skeleton scenes of the *Commedia dell' Arte*—for a dramatist may have his characters fully imagined, and still leave them as inexpressive as they might be in real life—that will allow the actor too much initiative. Actors who are in themselves interesting, lively and resourceful can make a passingly brilliant effect with such material. But, like other fairy gold, it will be dead leaves in the morning. The records of the theatre are choked with such empty, perished plays. The dramatist must not, on the other hand, try to do for the actor what the actor can do as well, and better, for himself.

E.E. Stoll on Hamlet's Delay

If such be the opinion of Hamlet in the seventeenth and eighteenth centuries, what way is there left to judge between them and us but to appeal to Shakespeare himself, and, as best we may, inquire what he intended. To the business of this inquiry we now turn.

The only fault, as we have seen, that the eighteenth century discovered, was, in so far as the two can be separated, in the play and not in the man. "The Poet ... was obliged to delay his Hero's Revenge," observes the author of *Some Remarks*; "but then he should have contrived some good Reason for it."[1] Though for this critic it was a matter of deficient motivation, he did not look for the motive in psychology. Yet to us, in our modern preoccupation with character, it would seem as if Shakespeare had deliberately manipulated his fable so as to place the motive there. Kyd himself had attempted to justify the delay. And he did this, if we are to take the evidence of the *Fratricide Punished* and the *Spanish Tragedy*, by three means: by introducing guards about the King to make access difficult; by turning the feigned madness to account to make access easier; and by giving an appropriate character to the hero. Of the three, Shakespeare employs only the last—characterization. In doing so the only motives presented for the delay are: the hero's aversion to the deed, but once directly expressed ("Oft cursed spite," etc.); his doubt of the Ghost; his desire to kill the King when engaged in some act of wickedness instead of when at prayer; and the cowardice and neglect of duty of which he vaguely and contradictorily accuses himself. (...)

How much the dramatist was bent on motiving the story without impairing the prestige of the hero appears from the nature of the reproach. "Forgetting" and "tardiness" are the burden of it. "Remember me," cries the Ghost at parting. "Do not forget," he adjures his son when he reappears to him in the Queen's bedchamber. "Tardy," "bestial oblivion," "letting all sleep,"—such are the charges that Hamlet brings against himself. He suffers capability and godlike reason to fust in him unused.[8] So it is with Hieronimo:—he calls himself "remisse"; Belimperia calls him "slacke"; and Isabella bewails his "negligence."[9] How much more it is a matter of story than of character, particularly this forgetting! Psychologically taken, how could Hamlet forget—"while memory holds a seat in this distracted globe"!—and remember anything else? But he remembers everything else, and is not oblivious, neglectful, or tardy, for all that you would expect him to be, in any other matter. As a motive or link in a story, however, the device, though a makeshift, is not uncommon. How, in real life, could Edgar, Albany, and the rest forget King Lear until Kent enters to remind them, or forget Cordelia until she is hanged? "Great thing of us forgot," cries Edgar;—and yet this thing was all that he cared for, and what was happening to Edmund and the demon sisters was nothing to him at all. But plot, tragic effect demanded that Cordelia should die, and that the entrance of Lear with her body should come only after the minor matters had been disposed of. Hence the dramatic and climactic postponement, the forgetting which explains it but (for us) needs itself to be explained. (...)

There is a defect in the drama, of course, but it is only as our technique is superimposed upon the drama that this is turned into a tragic defect in the hero, or that by his straightforward and magnanimous complaints and reproaches he is made to take the stand against himself. How far we go in this putting upon the older drama of the form and fashion of our own appears from the treatment recently given to the Orestes of the *Choephori*. Professor Wilamowitz-Moellendorff[13] finds traces of hesitation and unwillingness to do the deed in the long preliminary lamentations of the princely youth for his father and in the appeals to him and the gods. The reason is (though he does not say so) that otherwise they are for the critic not dramatic enough—being the mere utterance of emotion, simple lamentation, invocation, or prayer. To him, as to the Hamlet critics, the interval between the resolve and the deed must mean something—something inward and psychological. For the Greek it only made the deed more momentous. Such is the difference between the ancient (or Elizabethan) and the modern, between a Greek and a German. But it is a difference which it is the function of scholarship to mediate, a gulf which scholarship alone can bridge.

Notes

1. p. 33.

8. These expressions quite contradict the Coleridgean theory, as do the facts in the story. But to those who can treat the text as a document rather than as a play this circumstance presents no difficulty. "So sehr steht er unter dem Bann seiner Reflexion, dass er zu Zeiten glauben kann, er denke noch zu wenig—eine Erwagung die mich immer aufs Tiefste erschüttert" (Bulthaupt, ii, p. 248). That is, a soliloquy need not necessarily serve for the spectator's enlightenment, and a dramatist may as well put him on the wrong track as on the right.

9. See above, pp. 15–16 from *Hamlet: Historical and Comparative Study*; also, *Spanish Tragedy*. III, xiii, 106, 156.

13. In his translation of the *Choephori*, introduction, pp. 147–49.

HAROLD BLOOM ON HAMLET'S UNFULFILLED RENOWN

There are magnificent writers who have the highest spiritual ambitions: Dante, Milton, Blake. Shakespeare, like Chaucer and Cervantes, had other interests: primarily, in the representation of the human. Though Shakespeare perhaps ought not to have become a secular scripture for us, he does seem to me the only possible rival to the Bible, in literary power. Nothing, when you stand back from it, seems odder or more wonderful than that our most successful entertainer should provide an alternative vision (however unintentionally) to the accounts of human nature and destiny in the Hebrew Bible, the New Testament, and the Koran. Yahweh, Jesus, Allah, speak with authority, and in another sense so do Hamlet, Iago, Lear, and Cleopatra. Persuasiveness is larger in Shakespeare because he is richer; his rhetorical and imaginative resources transcend those of Yahweh, Jesus, and Allah, which sounds rather more blasphemous than I think it is. Hamlet's consciousness; and his language for extending that consciousness, is wider and more agile than divinity has manifested, as yet.

Hamlet has many enigmas; they will go on being uncovered, just as the theologians and mystics will continue to expound the mysteries of God. There is always less urgency in our meditations upon Hamlet than upon God, and yet I am tempted to remark of Hamlet what the ancient Gnostics affirmed about Jesus: first he resurrected, and *then* he died. The Hamlet of act 5 has risen from the dead self of the earlier Hamlet. It is the resurrected Hamlet who says "Let it be," rather than "To be or not to be." There are less subtle resurrections in the late romances; I know of nothing subtler in all literature than the transformation and apparent apotheosis of Hamlet. (...)

I have been chided by reviewers for suggesting that Shakespeare "invented the human," as we now know it. Dr. Johnson said that the essence of poetry was invention, and it should be no surprise that the world's strongest dramatic poetry should have so revised the human as pragmatically to have reinvented it. Shakespearean detachment, whether in the Sonnets or in Prince Hamlet, is a rather original mode. Like so many Shakespearean inventions, it has Chaucerian origins, but tends to outrun Chaucerian ironies. G. K. Chesterton, still one of my critical heroes, points out that Chaucer's humor is sly, but lacks the "wild fantasticality" of Hamlet. Chaucer's slyness, Chesterton remarks, is a kind of prudence, quite unlike Shakespearean wildness. I find that useful; Hamlet's wild detachment is another of the prince's quests for freedom: from Elsinore, and from the world. Even Chaucer's Wife of Bath, fierce and idiosyncratic, does not quest for Hamlet's wild freedom.

Hamlet speaks seven soliloquies; they have two audiences, ourselves and Hamlet, and we gradually learn to emulate him by overhearing rather than just hearing. We overhear, whether or not we are Hamlet, contrary to the speaker's awareness, perhaps even against the speaker's intention. Overhearing Yahweh or Jesus or Allah is not impossible, but is rather difficult, since you cannot become God. You overhear Hamlet by becoming Hamlet; that is Shakespeare's art in this most original of all his plays. Refusing identity with Hamlet is by now almost unnatural, particularly if you tend to be an intellectual. A number of actresses have played Hamlet. I wish that more would attempt the role. As a representation, Hamlet transcends maleness. He is the ultimate overhearer, and that attribute is beyond gender.

We tend to define "genius" as extraordinary intellectual power. Sometimes we add the metaphor of "creative" power to the definition. Of all fictive personages, Hamlet stands foremost in genius. Shakespeare gives copious evidence of the prince's intellectual strength. For the power of creation, we are given mostly equivocal signs, except for the Player-King's great speech, and the mad little songs Hamlet intones in the graveyard.

I suggest that the play *Hamlet* is a study in its protagonist's balked creativity, the prince's unfulfilled renown as a poet. My suggestion scarcely is original; it is implicit in William Hazlitt, and is central to Harold Goddard's interpretation of the drama. But I want to be as clear as I am capable of being; I do not mean that Hamlet was a failed poet, that being the French Hamlet of T S. Eliot. The Hamlet of the first four acts is balked by his father's ghost, that is to say, by the prince's partial and troubled, internalization of his father's spirit. In act 5, the Ghost has been exorcised, by a great creative effort that Shakespeare leaves largely implicit. The exorcism takes place at sea, in the interval between acts 4 and 5. Shakespeare, who generally seems the most open of all writers, can also be the most elliptical. He loves to be excessive—at putting things in, while he slyly also educates us by leaving things out. *Hamlet* is a huge play, and yet it is also a giant torso, with much, on purpose, omitted. How to read *Hamlet* is a challenge that touches a height in the transition between act 4 and act 5. Why read *Hamlet*? Because, by now, this play makes us an offer we cannot refuse. It has become our tradition, and the word our there is enormously inclusive. Prince Hamlet is the intellectual's intellectual: the nobility, and the disaster, of Western consciousness. Now Hamlet has also become the representation of intelligence itself, and that is neither Western nor Eastern, male nor female, black nor white, but merely the human at its best, because Shakespeare is the first truly multicultural writer. (…)

Hamlet as the Limit of Stage Drama

Shakespeare's only son, Hamnet, died at age eleven in 1596. John Shakespeare, the poet's father, died in 1601. At thirty-seven, Shakespeare had lost both. What ever relation this had to *Hamlet* has to be conjectural, and was most eloquently propounded by James Joyce's Stephen Dedalus in the Library scene of *Ulysses*:

> —*Sabellius, the African, subtlest heresiarch of all the beasts of the field, held that the Father was Himself His Own Son. The bulldog of Aquin, with whom no word shall be impossible, refutes him. Well: if the father who has not a son be not a father can the son who has not a father be a son? When Rutlandbaconsouthampton-shakespeare or another poet of the same name in the comedy of errors wrote* Hamlet *he was not the father of his own son merely but, being no more a son, he was and felt himself the father of all his race, the father of his own grandfather, the father of his unborn grandson who, by the same token, never was born....*

If *Hamlet* constitutes, to whatever degree, a meditation upon fathers and sons—and most of us agree with that notion—the context for dramatic brooding on filial matters is observed by the overt enigmas of stage representation. The black prince, a dramatic individual, comes to understand that he has been mourning the idea of fatherhood/sonship rather than the actual King Hamlet, an uxorious killing machine with whom the great soliloquist has absolutely nothing in common. When the Ghost, who seems to have undergone rather minimal character change in Purgatory, glides onto the closet scene, he still demands Claudius's blood. As in Act I, he is unconcerned with his son's well-being, but instead becomes alarmed at Gertrude's psychic condition. The prince, in the Ghost's view, is to be a sword of vengeance: no more nor less.

Shakespeare, despite much scholarly argument to the contrary, was no lover of authority, which had murdered Christopher Marlowe, tortured and broken Thomas Kyd, and branded Ben Jonson. The poet kept some distance from the ruling powers, and temporized whenever necessary. Are we to believe that Hamlet loves authority? He tries, but it will not work. Even the Ghost, supposed image of the play's only authentic authority, is soon enough addressed by his son as "truepenny" and "old mole," and referred to as "this fellow in the cellarage." Hamlet's mourning, of which we continue to make too much, has equivocal elements. Like Samuel Beckett, who wrote his own Hamlet in Endgame, the prince is sorrier for humankind than he is for himself.

You cannot reduce Hamlet to any consistency, even in his grief. His drama is limitless precisely because his personality is informed by his own cognitive power, which appears unbounded. Since, in Hamlet's case, the play *is* the figure, we pragmatically cannot hold this, of all Shakespeare's dramas, together in our minds. Samuel Johnson, properly puzzled and not enthralled, said, "We must allow to the tragedy of *Hamlet* the praise of variety." One agrees with Johnson's mordant observation: "The apparition left the regions of the dead to little purpose," for the plot cannot change Hamlet. Only Hamlet can, by hearing his own formulations, and then thinking himself beyond them. Not just the most experimental of plays, *Hamlet* truly is the graveyard of drama. Shakespeare escaped from *Hamlet* to write *Othello* and *King Lear*, *Macbeth* and *Antony and Cleopatra*, but no one else—playwright or novelist—quite gets out of that burial ground. Our deep subjectivity hovers there, its emblem the skull of Yorick.

Iago was the solution that Shakespeare's genius found to the impasse Hamlet constitutes. The prince would not deign to say, "For I am nothing if not critical." Iago constructs his own isolation; Hamlet already is isolation. Shakespeare uses Iago to get started again, but with no ambition to go beyond Hamlet, which may be impossible. Even where the prince has only the absurd (Osric) to comment upon, his commentary nevertheless transcends its own prophecy:

A did comply with his dug before a sucked it. Thus has he—and many more of the same bevy that I know the drossy age dotes on—only got the tune of the time and, out of an habit of encounter, a kind of yeasty collection, which carries them through and through the most fanned and winnowed opinions; and do not but blow them to their trial, the bubbles are out.

[V.ii.184–91]

Osric here stands in not only for a flock of contemporary courtiers, but for fashionable rival playwrights, and possibly for most of us as well, whoever we are. It is the dramatic placement of the Osric follies that startles: Hamlet is aware he is about to enter Claudius's last entrapment, in the duel with Laertes. To call his stance "insouciant" would undervalue it. As always, he mocks the play: plot, ethos, context.

Shakespeare partly answers Hamlet's irony by an enormous advance in the representations of villains: Iago, Edmund in *King Lear*, Macbeth. Extraordinary as these are, they do not bruise the demarcations between their plays and reality. Hamlet's undiscovered country, his embassy of annihilation, voids the limits that ought to confine his drama to stage dimensions.

A.C. BRADLEY ON THE EFFECTS OF HAMLET'S MELANCHOLY

Finally, Hamlet's melancholy accounts for two things which seem to be explained by nothing else. The first of these is his apathy or 'lethargy.' We are bound to consider the evidence which the text supplies of this, though it is usual to ignore it. When Hamlet mentions, as one possible cause of his inaction, his 'thinking too precisely on the event,' he mentions another, 'bestial oblivion'; and the thing against which he inveighs in the greater part of that soliloquy (IV. iv.) is not the excess or the misuse of reason (which for him here and always is god-like), but this *bestial* oblivion or '*dullness*,' this 'letting all *sleep*,' this allowing of heaven-sent reason to 'fust unused':

What is a man,
If his chief good and market of his time
Be but to *sleep* and feed ? a *beast*, no more.[1]

So, in the soliloquy in II. ii. he accuses himself of being 'a *dull*
and muddy-mettled rascal,' who 'peaks [mopes] like John-a-
dreams, unpregnant of his cause,' dully indifferent to his
cause.[2] So, when the Ghost appears to him the second time, he
accuses himself of being tardy and lapsed in *time*; and the
Ghost speaks of his purpose being almost *blunted*, and bids him
not to *forget* (cf. 'oblivion'). And so, what is emphasised in those
undramatic but significant speeches of the player-king and of
Claudius is the mere dying away of purpose or of love.[3] Surely
what all this points to is not a condition of excessive but useless
mental activity (indeed there is, in reality, curiously little about
that in the text), but rather one of dull, apathetic, brooding
gloom, in which Hamlet, so far from analysing his duty, is not
thinking of it at all, but for the time literally *forgets* it. It seems
to me we are driven to think of Hamlet *chiefly* thus during the
long time which elapsed between the appearance of the Ghost
and the events presented in the Second Act. The Ghost, in fact,
had more reason than we suppose at first for leaving with
Hamlet as his parting injunction the command, 'Remember
me,' and for greeting him, on reappearing, with the command,
'Do not forget.'[4] These little things in Shakespeare are not
accidents.

The second trait which is fully explained only by Hamlet's
melancholy is his own inability to understand why he delays.
This emerges in a marked degree when an occasion like the
player's emotion or the sight of Fortinbras's army stings
Hamlet into shame at his inaction. '*Why*,' he asks himself in
genuine bewilderment, 'do I linger? Can the cause be
cowardice? Can it be sloth? Can it be thinking too precisely of
the event? And does *that* again mean cowardice? What is it that
makes me sit idle when I feel it is shameful to do so, and when I
have *cause, and will, and strength, and means*, to act?' A man
irresolute merely because he was considering a proposed action

too minutely would not feel this bewilderment. A man might feel it whose conscience secretly condemned the act which his explicit consciousness approved; but we have seen that there is no sufficient evidence to justify us in conceiving Hamlet thus. These are the questions of a man stimulated for the moment to shake off the weight of his melancholy, and, because for the moment he is free from it, unable to understand the paralysing pressure which it exerts at other times.

I have dwelt thus at length on Hamlet's melancholy because, from the psychological point of view, it is the centre of the tragedy, and to omit it from consideration or to underrate its intensity is to make Shakespeare's story unintelligible. But the psychological point of view is not equivalent to the tragic; and, having once given its due weight to the fact of Hamlet's melancholy, we may freely admit, or rather may be anxious to insist, that this pathological condition would excite but little, if any, tragic interest if it were not the condition of a nature distinguished by that speculative genius on which the Schlegel–Coleridge type of theory lays stress. Such theories misinterpret the connection between that genius and Hamlet's failure, but still it is this connection which gives to his story its peculiar fascination and makes it appear (if the phrase may be allowed) as the symbol of a tragic mystery inherent in human nature. Wherever this mystery touches us, wherever we are forced to feel the wonder and awe of man's godlike 'apprehension' and his 'thoughts that wander through eternity,' and at the same time are forced to see him powerless in his petty sphere of action, and powerless (it would appear) from the very divinity of his thought, we remember Hamlet. And this is the reason why, in the great ideal movement which began towards the close of the eighteenth century, this tragedy acquired a position unique among Shakespeare's dramas, and shared only by Goethe's *Faust*. It was not that *Hamlet* is Shakespeare's greatest tragedy or most perfect work of art; it was that *Hamlet* most brings home to us at once the sense of the soul's infinity, and the sense of the doom which not only circumscribes that infinity but appears to be its offspring.

Notes

1. Throughout, I italicise to show the connection of ideas.

2. Cf. *Measure for Measure*, IV. iv. 23, 'This deed ... makes me unpregnant and dull to all proceedings.'

3. III. ii. 196 ff., iv. vii. III ff.: *e.g.*,
   Purpose is but the slave to memory,
   Of violent birth but poor validity.

4. So, before, he had said to him:
   And duller should'st thou be than the fat weed
   That roots itself in ease on Lethe wharf,
   Would'st thou not stir in this.

William Empson on Shakespeare's First Audiences

The real "Hamlet problem", it seems clear, is a problem about his first audiences. This is not to deny (as E. E. Stoll has sometimes done) that Hamlet himself is a problem; he must be one, because he says he is; and he is a magnificent one, which has been exhaustively examined in the last 150 years. What is peculiar is that he does not seem to have become one until the end of the eighteenth century; even Dr Johnson, who had a strong grasp of natural human difficulties, writes about Hamlet as if there was no problem at all. We are to think, apparently, that Shakespeare wrote a play which was extremely successful at the time (none more so, to judge by the references), and continued to hold the stage, and yet that nearly two hundred years had to go by before anyone had even a glimmering of what it was about. This is a good story, but surely it is rather too magical. Indeed, as the Hamlet Problem has developed, yielding increasingly subtle and profound reasons for his delay, there has naturally developed in its wake a considerable backwash from critics who say "But how can such a drama as you describe conceivably have been written by an Elizabethan, for an Elizabethan audience?" Some kind of mediating process is required here; one needs to explain how the first audiences could take a more interesting view than Dr Johnson's, without taking an improbably profound one.

The political atmosphere may be dealt with first. Stoll has successfully argued that even the theme of delay need not be grasped by an audience, except as a convention; however, Dover Wilson has pointed out that the first audiences had a striking example before them in Essex, who was, or had just been, refusing to make up his mind in a public and alarming manner; his attempt at revolt might have caused civil war. One need not limit it to Essex; the Queen herself had long used vacillation as a major instrument of policy, but the habit was becoming unnerving because though presumably dying she still refused to name a successor, which in itself might cause civil war. Her various foreign wars were also dragging on indecisively. A play about a prince who brought disaster by failing to make up his mind was bound to ring straight on the nerves of the audience when Shakespeare rewrote *Hamlet*; it is not a question of intellectual subtlety but of what they were being forced to think about already. It seems to me that there are relics of this situation in the text, which critics have not considered in the light of their natural acting power. The audience is already in the grip of a convention by which Hamlet can chat directly to them about the current War of the Theatres in London, and then the King advances straight down the apron-stage and urges the audience to kill Hamlet:

Do it, England,
For like the hectic in my blood he rages,
And *thou* must cure me.

None of them could hear that without feeling it was current politics, however obscure; and the idea is picked up again, for what seems nowadays only an opportunist joke, when the Gravedigger says that Hamlet's madness won't matter in England, where all the men are as mad as he. Once the idea has been planted so firmly, even the idea that England is paying Danegeld may take on some mysterious weight. Caroline Spurgeon and G. Wilson Knight have maintained that the reiterated images of disease somehow *imply* that Hamlet himself is a disease, and this gives a basis for it. Yet the audience might also reflect that the character does what the author is doing—altering an old play to fit an immediate political purpose. This had to be left obscure, but we can reasonably presume an idea that the faults of Hamlet (which are somehow part of his great virtues) are not only specific but, topical—"so far from being an absurd old play, it is just what you want, if you can see what is at the bottom of it". The insistence on the dangers of civil war, on the mob that Laertes does raise, and that Hamlet could raise but won't, and that Fortinbras at the end takes immediate steps to quiet, is rather heavy in the full text though nowadays often cut. Shakespeare could at least feel, when the old laughingstock was dragged out and given to him as a new responsibility, that delay when properly treated need not be dull; considered politically, the urgent thing might be not to let it get too exciting.

Such may have been his first encouraging reflection, but the political angle was not the first problem of the assignment, the thing he had to solve before he could face an audience; it was more like an extra gift which the correct solution tosses into his hand. (...)

The objection is not against melodrama, which they liked well enough, but against delay. You had a hero howling out "Revenge" all through the play, and everybody knew the revenge wouldn't come till the end. This structure is at the mercy of anybody in the audience who cares to shout "Hurry Up", because then the others feel they must laugh, however sympathetic they are; or rather, they felt that by the time Shakespeare rewrote *Hamlet*, whereas ten years earlier they would only have wanted to say "Shush". This fact about the audience, I submit, is the basic fact about the rewriting of *Hamlet*.

HAROLD C. GODDARD
ON HAMLET'S INDIVIDUALITY

When such a spacious mirror's set before him,
He needs must see himself.

I

There is no mystery in a looking glass until someone looks into it. Then, though it remains the same glass, it presents a different face to each man who holds it in front of him. The same is true of a work of art. It has no proper existence as art until someone is reflected in it—and no two will ever be reflected in the same way. However much we all see in common in such a work, at the center we behold a fragment of our own soul, and the greater the art the greater the fragment. *Hamlet* is possibly the most convincing example in existence of this truth. In a less "spacious mirror" it is often concealed or obscured. But "Hamlet wavered for all of us," as Emily Dickinson said, and everyone admits finding something of himself in the Prince of Denmark. *Hamlet* criticism seems destined, then, to go on being what it has always been: a sustained difference of opinion. It is quite as if *Hamlet* were itself a play within a play. *The Murder of Gonzago* was one thing to the Prince, another to the King, and others still to the Queen, Polonius, Ophelia, and the rest. So *Hamlet* is to us. The heart of its hero's mystery will never be plucked out. No theory of his character will ever satisfy all men, and even if one should convince one age, it would not the next. But that does not mean that a deep man will not come closer to that mystery than a shallow man, or a poetic age than a prosaic one—just as Hamlet saw more in "The Mouse-trap" than Rosencrantz or Guildenstern could conceivably have seen. No one but a dead man can escape projecting himself on the Prince of Denmark. But some will project themselves on many, others on only a few, of the innumerable facets of his personality. The former, compared with the latter, will obtain a relatively objective view of the man. And this process will continue to create what might be called the world's slowly growing portrait of Hamlet. Over the years the cairn of *Hamlet* criticism is more than any stone that has been thrown upon it.

II

To nearly everyone both Hamlet himself and the play give the impression of having some peculiarly intimate relation to their creator. What that relation may originally have been we shall probably never know. But it is hard to refrain from speculating. When we learn that Dostoevsky had a son, Alyosha (Alexey), whom he loved dearly and who died before he was three, and that the father began writing *The Brothers Karamazov* that same year, the temptation is irresistible to believe that its hero, Alexey Karamazov, is an imaginative reincarnation of the child, a portrayal of what the author would have liked the boy to become. In this instance the father bestowed an immortality that there is only a negligible chance the son would have achieved if he had lived. Shakespeare's son Hamnet died at the age of eleven, possibly not long before his father began to be attracted by the Hamlet story. Was there any connection? We do not know. But the name, in its interchangeable forms, must have had strong emotional associations for Shakespeare. Hamnet and Judith Sadler, neighbors and friends of the Shakespeares, were godparents to their twins, to whom they gave their names. When Shakespeare was sixteen, a girl, Katherine Hamlett, was drowned near Stratford under circumstances the poet may have remembered when he told of Ophelia's death. Resemblances between Hamlet and the Earl of Essex, who, in turn, figured significantly in Shakespeare's life, have frequently been pointed out.

However all this may be, there is no doubt that Shakespeare endowed Hamlet with the best he had acquired up to the time he conceived him. He inherits the virtues of a score of his predecessors—and some of their weaknesses. Yet he is no mere recapitulation of them. In hint, rather, they recombine to make a man as individual as he is universal. He has the passion of Romeo ("Romeo is Hamlet in love," says Hazlitt), the dash and audacity of Hotspur, the tenderness and genius for friendship of Antonio, the wit, wisdom, resourcefulness, and histrionic gift of Falstaff, the bravery of Faulconbridge, the boyish charm of the earlier Hal at his best, the poetic fancy of Richard II, the analogic power and meditative melancholy of Jaques, the idealism of Brutus, the simplicity and human sympathy of Henry VI, and, after the assumption of his antic disposition, the wiliness and talent for disguise of Henry IV and the cynicism and irony of Richard III—not to mention gifts and graces that stem more from certain of Shakespeare's heroines than from his heroes—for, like Rosalind, that inimitable boy–girl, Hamlet is an early draft of a new creature on the Platonic order, conceived in the *Upanishads*, who begins to synthesize the sexes. "He who understands the masculine and keeps to the feminine shall become the whole world's channel. Eternal virtue shall not depart from him and he shall return to the state of an infant." If Hamlet does not attain the consummation that Laotse thus describes, he at least gives promise of it.

WILLIAM HAZLITT ON THE CHARACTER OF HAMLET

Hamlet is a name; his speeches and sayings but the idle coinage of the poet's brain. What then, are they not real? They are as real as our own thoughts. Their reality is in the reader's mind. It is *we* who are Hamlet. This play has a prophetic truth, which is above that of history. Whoever has become thoughtful and melancholy through his own mishaps or those of others; whoever has borne about with him the clouded brow of reflection, and thought himself 'too much i' th' sun'; whoever has seen the golden lamp of day dimmed by envious mists rising in his own breast, and could find in the world before him only a dull blank with nothing left remarkable in it; whoever has known 'the pangs of despised love, the insolence of office, or the spurns which patient merit of the unworthy takes'; he who has felt his mind sink within him, and sadness cling to his heart like a malady, who has had his hopes blighted and his youth staggered by the apparitions of strange things; who cannot be well at ease, while he sees evil hovering near him like a spectre; whose powers of action have been eaten up by thought, he to whom the universe seems infinite, and himself nothing; whose bitterness of soul makes him careless of consequences, and who goes to a play as his best resource to shove off, to a second remove, the evils of life by a mock representation of them—this is the true Hamlet.

We have been so used to this tragedy that we hardly know how to criticise it any more than we should know how to describe our own faces. But we must make such observations as we can. It is the one of Shakespear's plays that we think of the oftenest, because it abounds most in striking reflections on human life, and because the distresses of Hamlet are transferred, by the turn of his mind, to the general account of humanity. Whatever happens to him we apply to ourselves, because he applies it so himself as a means of general reasoning. He is a great moraliser; and what makes him worth attending to is, that he moralises on his own feelings and experience. He is not a common-place pedant. If *Lear* is distinguished by the greatest depth of passion, HAMLET is the most remarkable for the ingenuity, originality, and unstudied developement of character. Shakespear had more magnanimity than any other poet, and he has shewn more of it in this play than in any other. There is no attempt to force an interest: every thing is left for time and circumstances to unfold. The attention is excited without effort, the incidents succeed each other as matters of course, the characters think and speak and act just as they might do, if left entirely to themselves. There is no set purpose, no straining at a point. The observations are suggested by the passing scene—the gusts of passion come and go like sounds of music borne on the wind. The whole play is an exact transcript of what might be supposed to have taken place at the court of Denmark, at the remote period of time fixed upon, before the modern refinements in morals and manners were heard of. It would have been interesting enough to have been admitted as a bystander in such a scene, at such a time, to have heard and witnessed something of what was going on. But here we, are more than spectators. We have not only 'the outward pageants and the signs of grief'; but 'we have that within which passes shew.' We read the thoughts of the heart, we catch the passions living as they rise. Other dramatic writers give us very fine versions and paraphrases of nature; but Shakespear, together with his own comments, gives us the original text, that we may judge for ourselves. This is a very great advantage.

The character of Hamlet stands quite by itself. It is not a character marked by strength of will or even of passion, but by refinement of thought and sentiment. Hamlet is as little of the hero as a man can well be: but he is a young and princely novice, full of high enthusiasm and quick sensibility—the sport of circumstances, questioning with fortune and refining on his own feelings, and forced from the natural bias of his disposition by the strangeness of his situation. He seems incapable of deliberate action, and is only hurried into extremities on the spur of the occasion, when he has no time to reflect, as in the scene where he kills Polonius, and again, where he alters the letters which Rosencraus and Guildenstern are taking with them to England, purporting his death. At other times when he is most bound to act, he remains puzzled, undecided, and sceptical, dallies with his purposes, till the occasion is lost, and finds out some pretence to relapse into indolence and thoughtfulness again. For this reason he refuses to kill the King when he is at his prayers, and by a refinement in malice, which is in truth only an excuse for his own want of resolution, defers his revenge to a more fatal opportunity, when he shall be engaged in some act 'that has no relish of salvation in it.'

> 'He kneels and prays,
> And now I'll do't, and so he goes to heaven,
> And so am I reveng'd: *that would be scann'd.*
> He kill'd my father, and for that,
> I, his sole son, send him to heaven.
> Why this is reward, not revenge.
> Up sword and know thou a more horrid time,
> When he is drunk, asleep, or in a rage.'

'Who's there?' says Barnardo, bravely, in the cold darkness on the castle platform. These are the first words of the play, and it is hard to see how they could be bettered. They carry, as often in Shakespeare, both an immediate meaning and a larger meaning, which is not simultaneously present but can grow in the mind as the play unfolds. Barnardo means only, 'Who goes there?', the sentry's challenge. The larger meaning is, 'Who is there, in the darkness, among the dead?' As I struggle to paraphrase, I find myself in danger of opting too easily for the more usual phrases: 'Is there life beyond grave?' 'Are there human existences on the far side of what we call death?' But these fail to take account of a certain grammatical peculiarity in Shakespeare's words; the sentry's challenge, though formally in the third person singular, is partly infiltrated by a sense of second person singular, arising from the fact that the question posed is addressed to its presumed subject. In which case we must modify our paraphrase, perhaps to 'Who, of you who are dead, is there?' The very awkwardness of the sentence is instructive. The English language naturally resists such a combination of second and third persons. Yet some such phrasing is needed, because *Hamlet* is not a cool treatise on death but is instead about an *encounter* with a dead person.

If Barnardo's words are to work at all, beyond their immediate sense, they must, so to speak, be set ticking, like a time bomb. All that is needed for this purpose is that the words be set slightly askew, so that the immediate meaning is felt to be in some degree unsatisfactory or incomplete. This is done, wonderfully, by Francisco's reply: 'Nay, answer me. Stand and unfold yourself!' Francisco means, "*I* am the sentry on duty, so I should be the one to issue the challenge. Now *you* tell me who *you* are." This exchange, with its wrong-footing of Barnardo, is remotely linked to farce, as many things will prove to be as the play goes on (two comic sentries frighten each other). But here the sense of fear is of course much stronger than any intuition of the ridiculous. We may think that Barnardo should formally have taken over from Francisco before challenging strangers, but the whole point of the challenge is that friend and foe cannot be distinguished at first. Shakespeare for once holds back on the theatrical metaphor—he does not make Francisco say, as the Volscian says in *Coriolanus* (IV.iii.48)[1]—'You take my part from me, sir'—but some sort of self-reference seems nevertheless to be going on: the actor arriving pat upon his cue matches neatly with 'most carefully upon your hour' (I.i.4) and 'Unfold yourself' is placed exactly to echo the other use of *unfold*: 'explain oneself to the audience; perform the exposition.' Thus we have fear, faintly absurd confusion and a question of identity, thrown out upon the dark. And all the while someone, or some thing—something other than Francisco—is there. At line 19 Horatio (if we follow the Second Quarto) or else Marcellus, shrewdly responding to the extra warmth of Barnardo's welcome, asks, 'What, has this thing appeared again tonight?'

Forty-six years ago in his Annual Shakespeare Lecture to the British Academy, C.S. Lewis said that the thing to remember about *Hamlet* is that it is about a man 'who has been given a task by a ghost'.[2] There is no ghost in Saxo Grammaticus's version of the Hamlet story, though there is in Belleforest's. We do not possess the Elizabeth *Hamlet* which preceded Shakespeare's, but we know form Lodge's reference to it that it contained a ghost. Curiously, we do possess Kyd's inverse *Hamlet*—for *The Spanish Tragedy* is about a father avenging his son—and there the whole action is watched by a dead man. In the *Ambales Saga* there are angels, and in remote Greek analogues there are, as we shall see, dreams, oracle and visions of a dead father. Hamlet in Shakespeare's play, is beckoned into the shadows by something which may be his father, may be the Devil, may even be, since our disorientation is so great, negation itself. He is then made party to the dark world, is changed utterly, cut off from marriage and friendship, made an agent of death. The Ghost tells him to wreak vengeance, but Hamlet notoriously finds himself strangely impeded. It is as if, having joined the shades, he finds himself drained of substance. He savages Opelia, because she is life, ready for procreation, but for the rest he is lost, suddenly adrift in the paralyzing liberty of a kind of solipsism; bounded by a nutshell he could count himself king of infinite space, but for his bad dreams (II. ii. 244). Such reality as persists figures, we notice, as mere nightmare to Hamlet.

'There is nothing either good or bad but thinking makes it so', he tells Rosencrantz and Guildenstern (II. Ii. 250-1). Professor Harold Jenkins in the New Arden edition robustly rejects the notion that ethical absolutes are here discarded, pointing out that the phrase is commonplace and has reference not to morals but to happiness or taste.[3] Certainly the same thought can be found (though not perhaps with precisely the same force) in Spenser and also in Montaigne, who knows it as a Stoic aphorism. But for all that, I sense that Professor Jenkins is here *too* robust. There was always a seed of epistemological relativism within Stoicism itself; the rational man is exhorted to rise above seeming misfortunes, bereavement, say, or exile, by exerting the power of reason, by reflecting that all must die, or that the good man is a citizen of the whole world and therefore cannot be exiled. One senses that reason is here being accorded, covertly, a fictive power to reconstruct reality according to the needs of the subject. Real reason, one feels, is an altogether more constrained affair. The Stoic philosopher in Johnson's *Rasselas*, when his daughter died, found the reality of loss simply insuperable: "What comfort," said the mourner, "can truth and reason afford me? Of what effect are they now, but to tell me, that my daughter will not be restored?"[4] Of course it is true that Stoicism with the major constraint of a rationally ordered cosmos is always present. With this, reason must always accord, and so by implication keep relativism at bay. But what of *Hamlet*, a Post-Stoic text? Surely it is not only bade readers who sense that now this thought is in suspension, hanging between ancient and modern conceptions. The passage taken as a whole is so instinct with a vertiginous uncertainty as to what is real, what unreal, what is waking, what dream, that the relativism germinally present even in Senecan Stoicism grows suddenly stronger. Philip Edwards in the New Cambridge edition[5] accepts Professor Jenkin's note, but only after a concessive clause: 'While this phrase voices an uncertainty about absolutes which reverberates through the play, Jenkins makes it clear ... ' and so on. The wilder meaning, which is as much epistemological as it is enthical, cannot be entirely excluded. (...)

The implied argument I have attached to the name of Wittgenstein works in this way: the very force of Hamlet, which must be at bottom a force of imagery, presupposes an intellectual softness, an impulse self-indulgently to tame the unimaginable with conventional pictures. This argument would, I suppose, have seemed strong to many philosophers in the 1950s and 1960s. But now philosophers seem less willing to dismiss as merely incoherent Hamlet's words 'There are more things in heaven and earth, Horatio, / Than are dreamt of in your philosophy' (I. v. 168-9). Perhaps it is the play, rather than twentieth-century philosophy, which perceives the full extent of our ignorance. If we do not know that death is any particular thing, equally we do not know that it excludes or is not any particular thing. If death is a sleep, there may be dreams in that sleep, and what kind of thing would that be ... ? Even today, in 1988, in clear daylight, do we know with confidence the answer to Barnardo's question: 'Who's there?'

The important question for a sixteenth-century mirror-gazer was not whether but why the image in the glass differed from the subject's ordinary impression. Was it dictated by a higher truth (moral judgment or superior models) or only by the subject's own distorting wishes? In the latter case he would be looking at a flattering glass rather than a true glass (the subject of the next chapter—) like Vanity in the emblem books, misled by worldly beauty. The important question about a dramatic mirror was like the one Hamlet found himself asking about the ghost: is this "thing" strange because it s revealing a hidden truth—or because some power is trying to deceive me? Is my father truly being murdered again on stage—(or, as Claudius might ask, "my brother")—or is it only a maliciously fictionalized version of that murder? Even if the spectators for Shakespeare's *Henry VI* were sophisticated enough.

Notes

1. All quotations from Shakespeare, are, unless otherwise specified, from William Shakespeare, *The Complete Works*, edited by Stanley Wells and Gary Taylor (Oxford: Clarendon Press, 1986).
2. Proceedings of the British Academy, 28 (1942), pp. 139–54, p. 147. Also in C. S. Lewis, *Selected Literary Essays* (Cambridge: Cambridge University Press, 1969), pp. 88–105, p. 97.
3. The New Arden edition of *Hamlet* (London: Methue, 1982), pp. 467–8.
4. *The History of Rasselas, Prince of Abyssinia*, ch. xviii, ed. Geoffrey Tillotson and Brian Jenkins (London: Oxford University Press, 1971), p. 51.
5. *Hamlet, Prince of Denmark*, the New Cambridge Shakespeare, ed. Philip Edwards (Cambridge: Cambridge University Press, 1985), p. 51.

FRANCIS FERGUSSON ON SHAKESPEARE'S REWORKING OF HIS SOURCES

Shakespeare wrote *Hamlet* in 1600, when he was thirty-six years old. The turn of the century is also an important turning point in Shakespeare's own career. He was already a skilled and experienced playwright. He had been a member of his own highly trained acting company for six years, and they had just acquired the Globe Theatre, which Shakespeare had helped to plan. He seems suddenly to have seen new and greater possibilities in the theater art which he had mastered. *Hamlet* (with *Julius Caesar*) begins his "tragic period" when, in the space of six or seven years, he wrote his greatest plays. (...)

In making *Hamlet* Shakespeare started with an old and popular story which he might have known from several sources. There are references to a Hamlet play several years before Shakespeare's, but that play is lost, and we do not know who wrote it, or whether Shakespeare made any use of it. He must have read Belleforest's *Histoires Tragiques* (1576), which includes the story as told by Saxo Grammaticus, a twelfth-century

Danish chronicler. It tells of a prince whose uncle has murdered his father and married his mother; who dedicates himself to vengeance; and who feigns madness to conceal his intentions from his uncle. That is the basis of Shakespeare's play, but the whole feeling is different: it looks like a good scenario for a typical Elizabethan "revenge play," like Kyd's *Spanish Tragedy*, which is often thought to be a forerunner of *Hamlet*. Shakespeare himself had written what is often called a revenge play, *Titus Andronicus*, at the very beginning of his career. But in dramatizing the tale for his own company and his own audience he brought the melodramatic plot, the Danish setting, and all the characters up to date. Hamlet has nothing in common with Saxo's primitive savage. With his doubts and his fears, he must have looked perfectly contemporary to the "super-subtle Elizabethans" of the worried days of the end of Elizabeth's reign. He still looks modern to us, in our time of troubles. And the other characters are also part of the familiar "modern" picture. Who has not met a good, old, boring Polonius, for instance, or a pair of sleek time-servers like Rosencrantz and Guildenstern?

In the imaginative process of embodying the old story in a modern setting, Shakespeare transformed the "revenge" motive, which is so simple in Saxo, into something much more significant. Sir Israel Gollancz has shown that the legendary figure of Hamlet (under various names) is to be found in Scandinavian tales and in the Roman myth of Brutus the Fool, who rid his country of the tyrannical Tarquins. Gilbert Murray thinks that the ultimate source is probably the same prehistoric rites of spring that gave rise to classic myths of the Orestes type. Murray points out many parallels between Orestes and Hamlet; and Hamlet is certainly more like Orestes than he is like Saxo's oafish chieftain. Orestes, like Hamlet, is a dispossessed king's son, whose father was murdered by his mother and her lover, and Orestes, like Hamlet, feels that it is up to him to set things right. His motive, as we see him in Greek tragedy, is more than simple revenge: he feels a religious obligation to restore order in his household and his community, and the Chorus, expressing the traditional beliefs of the people, accepts him as destined to purify the common moral life. He might have exclaimed, like Hamlet, "The time is out of joint; O cursed spite / That ever I was born to set it right." Of course when Hamlet feels his destiny upon him, he is not thinking of Orestes. And there is no reason to suppose that Shakespeare was either, or that he had any notion of the ancient sources of the story. But in exploring the possibilities in Saxo's tale he seems to have found, once more, the classic theme, which is also a very modern theme.

However that may be, this theme of the illness of the state, and of the young prince who is "born" or destined to cure it, is clearly the basis of the play as a whole. Shakespeare came to it by way of the nine history plays which he had written before *Hamlet*. In the history plays, the central theme is always the welfare of the English monarchy, which is torn by the civil wars of Lancaster and York, struggling for the crown. England was "ill" with dissension until the Tudors cured it; that is the theme which commanded the passionate interest of his patriotic audiences. And in *Hamlet* he makes it clear, at the very beginning, that that play also is to be about Denmark's illness and its cure. In scene 1, the soldiers, on guard on the castle parapet, fear war or some other external danger. When the Ghost appears for the second time, they realize that the danger is closer to home and more troublesome: it "bodes some strange eruption to our state." That is before Hamlet, the unfortunate young man fated to clear up the malady, has appeared. When he does appear, in scene 2, he also expresses the dangerous decay of the state before the Ghost has told him the facts of his father's murder and given him his terrible assignment:

Fie on't, ah fie, 'tis an unweeded garden
That grows to seed, things rank and gross in nature
Possess it merely.

After the prologue scenes, the main conflict, that between Hamlet and his uncle, King Claudius, develops quickly. It is a dynastic struggle, like those in the history plays. But because the stakes are the crown, and therefore Denmark itself, all of the characters are involved in it. Laertes depends on the King for his conventional fling in Paris; Fortinbras, in Norway, has some claim to the throne. Gertrude and Ophelia are involved through Hamlet, Claudius, and Polonius, and at last destroyed by the conflicts between them. Polonius is a natural "pillar of society," the tool of anyone who is king. The cynical courtiers live off of Denmark; the Danish people, whom Laertes stirs to rebellion in Act IV, the gravediggers in Act V, all suffer from and illustrate the Danish corruption. As soon as one realizes that the play is about Denmark and its hidden malady, all of the varied characters, the interwoven stories, and the contrasting effects of comedy, terror, and pathos which compose *Hamlet* fall naturally into place. It has been called a "Gothic tragedy," and, in fact, since it pictures a whole society, it is (like other great works of Renaissance art) composed on medieval principles. In its complex order, as in a Gothic cathedral, there is a place for heroes, for saints, and for gargoyles too.

CHARLES R. FORKER ON THE FUNCTION OF THEATRICAL SYMBOLISM

A rapid glance at any concordance will reveal that Shakespeare, both for words and metaphors, drew abundantly from the language of the theatre. Terms like *argument*, *prologue*, *stage*, *pageant*, *scene*, *player*, *act*, *actor*, *show*, *audience*, *rant*—these and their cousins that evoke dramatic connotations occur again and again throughout his plays in instances that range from very literal or technical significations to highly figurative and symbolic ones. This constant recourse to dramatic vocabulary suggests an analogy in Shakespeare's mind between life and the theatre—an analogy that he himself makes explicit and that even the name of his own theatre, the Globe, reinforces. Examples are not far to seek. Everyone will recall the famous reference of Jaques ("All the world's a stage" [*As You Like It*, II.vii.138]) and Macbeth ("Life's but a walking shadow, a poor player / That struts and frets his hour upon the stage"

[*Macbeth*, V.v.24–25]); and there are many others. Not infrequently the figure is associated with pain or death and the relation of man to the cosmos; hence, it becomes a natural focus for the idea of tragedy. The banished Duke in *As You Like It* speaks of the world as a "universal theatre" that "Presents more woeful pageants than the scene / Wherein we play" (II.vii.136–138); Lear with the penetration of madness bewails that "we are come / To this great stage of fools" (*King Lear*, IV.vi.182–183); and Richard of Bordeaux, the actor-king, glances back over his life to find it as unreal and as temporary as a play—"a little scene, / To monarchize, be fear'd, and kill with looks" (*Richard II*, Ill. ii.164–165).[1]

That Shakespeare should have conceived of man as an actor, the world as a stage, and the universe as its backdrop is not extraordinary, for, apart from the fact that he himself played the triple role of actor, playwright, and part owner of a theatre, the metaphor was of course a Renaissance commonplace. The motto of the Globe, *"Totus mundus agit histrionem,"* is only the most succinct expression of an idea extended to greater length in Montaigne, in Erasmus's *Praise of Folly*, in Romei's *Courtier's Academie*, and in the works of Shakespeare's fellow dramatists, as, for instance, the induction to Marston's *Antonio and Mellida*.[2]

The intention of this essay is to analyze some of the elaborate ramifications of the theatre symbol as it functions throughout *Hamlet*, to suggest that by reexamining the play with emphasis on the theme of acting, we may reach certain new perceptions about its dramatic architecture and see some of its central issues (Hamlet's delay, for instance, his disillusionment and madness, his intrigue with Claudius. his relation to his mother, his knowledge of himself) in fresh perspective. (...)

In *Hamlet* this duality functions almost constantly, not only because there is so much reference to playing and to related aspects of the fictional world, both literally and figuratively, but because the center of the play itself is largely concerned with the arrival of the players at Elsinore and the "mouse-trap" that constitutes the climax or turning point of the plot.[4] Since

Hamlet as a dramatic character is manifestly interested in the aesthetics of drama and its analogy to his own emotional predicament ("What's Hecuba to him, or he to Hecuba?" [II.ii.559]), the conflicts generated are teasingly complex. The theatrical references urge us to a sympathetic union with the characters, their actions and their feelings, and at the same time give them the objective reality of artifice through aesthetic distance. The world of the play becomes at once both more and less real than the actual world, and we are required to be aware of this relationship inside as well as outside the play.

The idea of theatre therefore embodies one of the mysterious paradoxes of tragedy, the impingement of appearance and reality upon each other. This is the very problem that obsesses Hamlet throughout the play and that eventually destroys both guilty and innocent alike. What is real seems false and what is false seems real. Spiritual growth, Shakespeare seems to say, is an extended lesson in separating out the components of the riddle and in learning to recognize and cope with one in the "role" or "disguise" of the other. Hence the theatre to Hamlet, to Shakespeare, and to the audience becomes a symbol for making unseen realities seen, for exposing the secret places of the human heart and objectifying them in a way without which they would be unbearable to look upon. We see into ourselves, as it were, through a looking glass. Thus the minor image is connected in Hamlet's mind with acting and, by extension, with other forms of art that penetrate hypocrisy and pretense: "the purpose of playing ... is, to hold, as 't were, the mirror up to nature, to show virtue her feature, scorn her own image, and the very age and body of the time his form and pressure" (III.ii.20–24). Later in the closet scene Hamlet verbally acts out his mother's crimes before her and teaches her by means of "counterfeit presentment" (III.iv.55) the difference between Hyperion and a satyr: "You go not till I set you up a glass / Where you may see the inmost part of you" (III.iv.20–21). In Ophelia's description of Hamlet as "The glass of fashion and the mold of form, / Th' observ'd of all observers" (III.i.156–157), the mirror and actor images coalesce as a symbol of truth reflected.

The very court of Denmark is like a stage upon which all the major characters except Horatio take parts, play roles, and practice to deceive. The irony is that Hamlet himself must adopt a pose in order to expose it in others. All the world's a stage. But for him pretense may entail revelation; Claudius "acts" only to conceal. Since, for Hamlet, the end of playing is to show virtue her feature and scorn her own image, he not only sees through false appearances ("Seems, madam! Nay, it is. I know not 'seems'" [I.ii.76]) but also feigns in order to objectify his inner feelings; he both uses and recognizes "honest" artifice. He welcomes the players enthusiastically and approves their art. One piece in their repertory, part of which he has memorized, he chiefly loves because there is "no matter in the phrase that might indict the author of affectation." It shows "an honest method, as wholesome as sweet" (II.ii.442–444). His antic disposition, although a smoke screen to protect him from his enemies, is also a dramatic device that allows Hamlet to express to himself and to the audience the nagging pain and disgust that the world of seeming has thrust upon him. It is by acting himself that he penetrates the "acts" of Polonius, of Rosencrantz and Guildenstern, of Gertrude, and even of the innocent Ophelia, upon whom her father has forced a role of duplicity.

Notes

1. Stage-consciousness and theatrical self-reference as prominent aspects of Elizabethan dramatic convention have been variously explored by many scholars. See, for instance, Reuben Brower, "The Mirror of Analogy: *The Tempest*," in *The Fields of Light* (New York: Oxford University Press, 1951), pp. 95–122; Anne Righter, *Shakespeare and the Idea of the Play* (London: Chatto and Windus, 1962); Clifford Lyons, "Stage Imagery in Shakespeare's Plays," in *Essays on Shakespeare and Elizabethan Drama in Honor of Hardin Craig*, ed. Richard Hosley (Columbia: University of Missouri Press, 1962), pp. 261–274; Herbert Weisinger, "Theatrun Mundi: Illusion as Reality," in *The Agony and the Triumph* (East Lansing: Michigan State University Press, 1964), pp. 58–70; Thomas B. Stroup, *Microcosmos: The Shape of the Elizabethan Play* (Lexington: University of Kentucky Press, 1965); Norman Rakbin, "The Great Globe Itself," in *Shakespeare and the Common Understanding* (New

York: Free Press, 1967), pp. 192–233; Jackson I. Cope, "The Rediscovery of Anti-Form in the Renaissance," *Comparative Drama*, 2 (1968), 155–171; Thelma N. Greenfield, *The Induction in Elizabethan Drama* (Eugene: University of Oregon Books, 1969); James L. Calderwood, *Shakespearean Metadrama* (Minneapolis: University of Minnesota Press, 1971) and Metadrama in *Shakespeare's Henriad* (Berkeley: University of California Press, 1979); Robert Egan, *Drama within Drama*: Shakespeare's Sense of His Art in "King Lear." "The Winter's Tale," and "The Tempest" (New York: Columbia University Press, 1975); and Coburn Freer, *The Poetics of Jacobean Drama* (Baltimore: Johns Hopkins University Press, 1981). See also chap. 3, n. 3.

For Shakespeare's awareness of his own craft with particular reference to *Hamlet*, see especially Maynard Mack, "The World of *Hamlet*," *Yale Review*, 41 (1952), 502–523;G. C. Thayer, "*Hamlet*: Drama as Discovery and as Metaphor," *Studia Neophilologica*, 28 (1956), 118–129; Richard Foster, "Hamlet and the Word," *University of Toronto Quarterly*, 30 (1961), 229–245; and Alvin B. Kernan, "Politics and Theatre in Hamlet," *Hamlet Studies*, 1 (1979), 1–12.

2. The theatrical trope is ancient. *Ernst Robert Curtius in European Literature and the Latin Middle Ages*, trans. W. R. Trask (New York: Pantheon Books, 1953), pp. 138–144, traces its permutations from Plato to Hofmannsthal.

4. Properly speaking, the device of play-within-play adds another plane of reality, making the response a triple or (if the anagogical level is included) a quadruple one. Looked at in this way, and gradations of actuality resemble a Platonic ladder, for the play-within-play is an image of an image. Real actors pretend to be actors entertaining an actor-audience, who, in turn, entertain a real audience, who are metaphorically actors on the world's stage and hence "walking shadows" of an ultimate cosmic reality of which they are but dimly aware. In reverse, the movement can be graphed as follows: ULTIMATE REALITY → ACTUAL WORLD → PLAY WORLD → PLAY-WITHIN-PLAY WORLD.

BERT O. STATES ON THE NATURE
OF HAMLET'S MELANCHOLY

There are two ways of thinking about melancholy—as a character trait and as a state of mind. As a trait, it would amount to a permanently gloomy disposition—how gloomy would depend on how central—something the individual carries around with him, like the black cloud over the head of the character in Al Capp's *L'il Abner*. Jaques, in *As You Like It* (where the word is used more than in any other Shakespeare play), would fit the disposition, and so would Don John in *Much Ado*, simply because there is no suggestion that either character had ever been anything but melancholy. Considered as a psychic state, however, melancholy might be either permanent or temporary, depending on how lucky the person was, in any case, it would be a dysfunction or a "malady" brought on, in all likelihood, by a massive reaction to experience, or, as the Elizabethans would assume, a poor mixture of the body humors. The only way, again, that you can tell one from the other is the manner in which the play treats the character. For example, one might argue that Jaques is really putting on a pose of melancholy, as Hamlet puts on the pose of an antic disposition, and that somewhere under the melancholy mask there is a character of a different sort. But there is no more characterological evidence for this assumption than there is that Jonson's characters are faking their greed or that Pinter's characters lead normal happy lives apart from their mendacious behavior in the plays.

In Hamlet's case, melancholy could hardly be called a trait. The play makes it amply clear that Hamlet's gloomy state of mind is not an old complaint but something brought on by recent events ("I have, of late, but wherefore I know not, lost all my mirth...."). And indeed, the events themselves, as Eliot pointed out, do not explain why Hamlet should fall into a melancholy, while another might not, but that is not an issue we need raise here. By everyone's observation, Hamlet is not himself:

> Sith nor th'exterior nor the inward man
> Resembles that it was. What it should be,
> More than his father's death, that thus hath put him
> So much from th'understanding of himself
> I cannot dream of.
>
> (2.2.6–10)

Here, and elsewhere, we are invited to imagine a Hamlet *they* know—or knew—but *we* don't. We are put in the position of projecting a character gestalt minus some of its key parts—as when someone says to you of a sad man, "He was such a happy man before she left him," you try to translate the sadness you see into the happiness you don't. And clearly this can be done. For a person who is newly or temporarily sad is sad in a provisional way and it is one of the mysteries of character that you can tell this after a brief exposure. Any single trait, or quality of behavior, functions synecdochically. You don't simply see sadness: you see a behavioral whole from which you can mentally extract sadness. Moreover, by an astonishing cognitive act of feature selection you are able to perceive that sadness, or cruelty, or gaiety are not central features of a personality— unless they happen to be—but auxiliary ones. They are not so much causal as caused, in somewhat the same sense that erratic firing is not a central trait of a combustion engine. (...)

One can hardly agree more, and much the same thing might be said of modern psychoanalytic readings of Hamlet's character— say, Lacan's Hamlet in search of his phallus—not to mention any reading motivated by an ideological point of view. But there is another way to look at the matter. What is it in Hamlet's character, as perceived (in 1942 or in 1991), that might lead someone to say that Hamlet was formerly a man of sanguine character, now a sufferer of melancholy adust? Is it not a case of putting the fictional character against the "chaotic jumble of ambiguous or contradictory fact and theory" (Forest, p. 656) of Renaissance medicine and allowing "the living example," so to speak, to serve as a biased selector of traits from the jumble itself? The truth is that Hamlet's moods do swing "back and forth" and that melancholy is the one humor in which this is a prominent symptom. Indeed, melancholy is the swinging sickness, whatever else may attend its onset, and there is a certain "logic" in Hamlet's behavior that is explained by no better word or concept than melancholy. Melancholy feeds on the other humors, swinging from intense excitement, anger, or irascibility—in a word, cruelty—to deep depression. As Robert Burton, and others, maintain, it "may be engendered of all four humours"; that is, it may "proceed" from choler, from phlegm, from blood ("which is the best")[2], and of course from itself (p. 342). The worst form of melancholy would be that proceeding from the adustion, or burning, of choler. From our post-Romantic viewpoint, this is what might be called unmelancholic melancholy, or manic melancholy, and as Foucault reminds us in *Madness and Civilization*, mania and melancholy have persistent affinities in the history of madness. There is in melancholy, he writes, "a kind of dialectic of qualities which, free from any constraint of substance, from any predetermination, makes its way through reversals and contradictions."[3] The frequent analogy for this merger of paralysis and fury is that of smoke to fire, melancholy serving as "a kind of wick or snuff," as Claudius might say, that abates the flame of the mania that produces it. Melancholy is potential cruelty, or cruelty coming; it is already self-cruelty, but it becomes cruelty to others when, under sufficient agitation, the stock melancholic response to the world, "Go away, I want to be alone!" is inflamed to "Go away or I'll kill you!"

If Shakespeare intended to portray melancholy in Hamlet, it is not the sort that we find elsewhere in the plays. It is impossible to determine, on strictly medical grounds, what Shakespeare was trying to portray in Hamlet's state of mind.[4] But whatever one calls it, it is not the "sighing sickness," or the Keatsean "wakeful anguish of the soul," or the French "vague du passion" that become so characteristic in the nineteenth century and continue into the twentieth in songs like "Melancholy Baby." Hamlet's complaint is an oscillation, but it is also a perceptual unity in which one "vole" contains the promise of the other, like one shoe dropping.

Notes

2. Robert Burton, *The Anatomy of Melancholy*, ed. Floyd Dell and Paul Jordan-Smith (London: Routledge, 1931), p. 152.

3. Michel Foucault, *Madness and Civilization: A History of Insanity in the Age of Reason*, trans. Richard Howard (New York: Random House, 1973), p.120.

4. Perhaps we can conclude this question of whether Shakespeare was actively following Elizabethan doctrines of physiology in the words of Paul Gottsshalk, one of the sanest and most generous-minded adjudicators of Shakespeare criticism: "Had it been Shakespeare's intention to imitate the conventions of one of these humors, he would have made the symptoms clear, whereas Hamlet's symptoms are as vague, from the point of view of Elizabethan physiology, as the term 'melancholy' itself.... If Shakespeare was attempting to portray such a type, then *Hamlet* is a failure in communication" (*The Meanings of "Hamlet": Modes of Literary Interpretation since Bradley* [Albuquerque: University of New Mexico Press, 1972], pp. 42–43). However, we might cite here Bridget Gellert Lyons's study of the symptoms of melancholy in Hamlet as one which treats the "conventions" of the condition, as they were presumably understood in Shakespeare's day, without insisting that Shakespeare was consciously drawing a physiological portrait:

"What makes Shakespeare's treatment of melancholy so much richer and more successful than that of any other dramatist is that in his hands the devices for representing it become expressive as well as dramatically functional.... Furthermore, Shakespeare has extended the range and complexity of melancholy as metaphor by making it include both the good and bad features of the condition" ("Melancholy and *Hamlet*," in *Voices of Melancholy: Studies in Literary Treatments of Melancholy in Renaissance England* [New York: Barnes & Noble, 1971], p. 78).

JOHN WILDERS PREFACE TO *HAMLET*

'If the dramas of Shakespeare were to be characterized, each by the particular excellence which distinguishes it from the rest,' wrote the first great English literary critic Samuel Johnson in 1765, 'we must allow to the tragedy of *Hamlet* the praise of variety.' Certainly this is the feature which distinguishes it from Shakespeare's other three major tragedies, and is one of the reasons why it has been a consistently popular play with theatre audiences. In *Othello* our attention is centered almost entirely on the psychological relationship between the two major characters; in *King Lear* on the extreme emotional pain suffered by the King, and in *Macbeth* on the moral disintegration of the hero. But, although our interest is always directed towards Hamlet (and in the few scenes from which he is absent he is the topic of conversation), nevertheless we are constantly seeing him in fresh kinds of situation and reacting to fresh kinds of people. The Prince dominates the foreground of the play but the background is filled with a large number and variety of other characters—Claudius, Polonius, Ophelia, the Player King, the Gravedigger, Osric—each one of whom has a strongly distinctive personality and speaks in a unique, characteristic style. This copious variety of character and style is a feature of some of the plays which Shakespeare had written during the years which preceded *Hamlet* (1601), especially the two parts of *Henry IV*. Hence, although the hero is always in the forefront of our minds, and the action is almost wholly confined to Elsinore, where he seems to be trapped (as Othello is apparently trapped with Iago in Cyprus, and Macbeth in Dunsinane), the audience is always being refreshed by changes of situation whether it be supernatural portents, the arts of acting and horsemanship, love, madness, death, or the ethics of suicide and revenge. One of Shakespeare's problems as he wrote this play must have been how to control and shape the potentially chaotic mass of material produced by his imagination. The limits of the three later tragedies are much more severely defined, though they are not for that reason the better plays.

The sheer variety of *Hamlet* is, presumably, not the only reason why it has been popular. The personality of the hero is the most complex in the whole of drama, and to attempt the role is the most testing challenge an actor can undertake. Hamlet adopts himself to every person and situation he meets and, hence, every character has a different opinion of him. With Claudius he is impertinent, with Rosencrantz and Guildenstern alternately genial and bitter, with Horatio affectionate, with the players courteous, with Ophelia full of pity, with Gertrude outraged, and with himself baffled and self-lacerating. He is ruminative in the graveyard, hysterical after the performance of the play, and stoical as he accepts the challenge to the fencing match. Since every actor is inclined to emphasize those characteristics with strike him most forcibly, it is not surprising that there have been as many different Hamlets as there have been players to interpret him. His ceaseless changes of mood are a sign of his emotional instability but they are also a deliberate attempt to baffle, and he has succeeded in perplexing the critics as well as the other characters.

He is also 'the melancholy Dane', and his particular kind of melancholy may also explain why generations of readers have found him sympathetic and absorbing. When he first appears he is, we learn, a man who has recently and radically changed. Before the play opened he had been, as Ophelia says,

> The courtier's, soldier's, scholar's eye, tongue, sword;
> Th' expectancy and rose of the fair state,
> The glass of fashion and the mould of form,
> Th' observed of all observers.

So variously has Shakespeare endowed the Prince's character that we can visualize the man he used to be without having seen him. Ophelia's praise does not seem excessive. By the time the play beings, however, he is already in a state of shocked disenchantment with human nature, for which he feels only disgust and disappointment:

> How weary, stale, flat and unprofitable,
> Seem to me all the uses of this world!
> Fie on't! Ah fie! 'tis an unweeded garden,
> That grows to see; things rank and gross in nature
> Possess it merely.

The cause of this disillusionment, as he goes on to reveal, is in the first place his mother's remarriage, an act which has affected him profoundly for several reasons. Coming so swiftly after her first husband's death, Gertrude's remarriage seems to him to show a callous indifference to his father's memory, and her former expressions of love now appear false and hypocritical. Moreover by marrying in middle age a palpably inferior man, she has revealed a desire for sexual gratification which her son finds repellent. As a result of what Hamlet sees as a betrayal of trust by the woman most intimately related to him, he becomes disenchanted with her, with women in general, and with humanity. In his first soliloquy he expresses a sense of outrage at the discrepancy between what his mother seemed to be, an ideally devoted wife, and what in his eyes she is, a faithless and incestuous woman. Hence he begins to doubt the certainty of all outward appearances, to feel he inhabits a world he can no longer trust, and he singles himself out as the only honest man in an otherwise dissembling world:

Seems, madam! Nay it is; I know not seems.

So movingly is Hamlet's melancholy expressed and so acute is his analysis of the other characters that it is tempting to assume that he is Shakespeare's own spokesman, the expression of the playwright's own disenchantment, and to look at the play through his eyes. But though Hamlet is sharply perceptive, the psychological shock he has suffered has also distorted his vision of other people. The violent expressions of disgust with which he assaults his mother, and particularly Ophelia, are scarcely deserved. Hamlet is at the same time more penetrating and more unbalanced than the other characters. Shakespeare allows us to understand him but also to judge him.

ARTHUR KIRSCH ON HAMLET'S GRIEF

HAMLET IS A REVENGE PLAY, and judging by the number of performances, parodies, and editions of *The Spanish Tragedy* alone, the genre enjoyed an extraordinary popularity on the Elizabethan stage. Part of the reason for that popularity is the theatrical power of the revenge motif itself. The quest for vengeance satisfies an audience's most primitive wishes for intrigue and violence. "The Tragic Auditory," as Charles Lamb once remarked, "wants blood,"[1] and the revenge motif satisfies it in abundance. Equally important, it gives significant shape to the plot and sustained energy to the action, whatever moral calculus one may use in judging the ethos of revenge itself.[2] But if vengeance composes the plot of the revenge play, grief composes its essential emotional content, its substance. In Marlowe's *Jew of Malta*, when Ferneze finds the body of his son killed in a duel, he cries out in his loss that he wishes his son had been murdered so that he could avenge his death.[3] It is a casual line, but it suggests a deep connection between anger and sorrow in the revenge-play genre itself that both Kyd and Shakespeare draw upon profoundly. At the end of *The Spanish Tragedy* the ghost of Andrea says, "Ay, now my hopes have end in their effects, / When blood and sorrow finish my desires" (4.5.1–2),[4] and it was unquestionably Kyd's brilliance in representing the elemental power of sorrow, as well as of blood, that enabled the revenge genre to establish so large a claim on the Elizabethan theatrical imagination. The speeches in which Hieronimo gives voice to his grief, including the famous "Oh eyes, no eyes, but fountains fraught with tears; / Oh life, no life, but lively form of death" (3.2.1–2) were parodied for decades after their first performance, so great was their impact, and the moving figure of an old man maddened with grief over the loss of his son was a major part of Shakespeare's theatrical inheritance.

In Shakespeare's play it is Hamlet himself who talks explicitly of sorrow and blood, relating them directly to the ghost as well as to each other in the scene in his mother's bedchamber in which the ghost appears for the last time. "Look you," he tells his mother, who characteristically cannot see the ghost,

> how pale he glares.
> His form and cause conjoined, preaching to stones,
> Would make them capable. (*To the Ghost*) Do not look upon me,
> Lest with this piteous action you convert
> My stern effects. Then what I have to do
> Will want true colour—tears perchance for blood
>   (3.4.116–21)

These lines suggest synapses between grief and vengeance that can help make the whole relation between the plot and emotional content of *Hamlet* more intelligible, and that particularly can help answer the charge made by many distinguished critics that Hamlet's emotions seem in excess of any objective cause as well as of the plot. T.S. Eliot's remark, for example, that Hamlet's mother is not an adequate equivalent for his disgust with her, that no possible action can satisfy this disgust, and that therefore "nothing that Shakespeare can do with the plot can express Hamlet for him" are at least susceptible to an answer if we take seriously Hamlet's own focus upon the experience of grief and upon its profound interaction with his task of revenge.[5]

The note of grief is sounded by Hamlet in his first words in the play, before he ever sees the ghost, in his opening dialogue with the King and his mother. The Queen says to him:

> Good Hamlet, cast thy nightly colour off,
> And let thine eye look like a friend on Denmark.
> Do not for ever with thy vailèd lids
> Seek for thy noble father in the dust.
> Thou know'st 'tis common—all that lives must die,
> Passing through nature to eternity.   (1.2.68–73)

Hamlet answers, "Ay, madam, it is common." "If it be / Why seems it so particular with thee?" she asks; and he responds,

> Seems, madam? Nay, it is. I know not "seems."
> 'Tis not alone my inky cloak, good-mother,
> Nor customary suits of solemn black,
> Nor windy suspiration of forced breath,
> No, nor the fruitful river in the eye,
> Nor the dejected haviour of the visage,
> Together with all forms, moods, shows of grief,
> That can denote me truly. These indeed "seem,"
> For they are actions that a man might play;
> But I have that within which passeth show—
> These but the trappings and the suits of woe. (1.2.74–86)

Though Hamlet's use of the conventional Elizabethan forms of mourning expresses his hostility to an unfeeling court, he is at the same time speaking deeply of an experience that everyone who has lost someone close to him must recognize. He is speaking of the early stages of grief, of its shock, of its inner and still hidden sense of loss, and trying to describe what is not fully describable—the literally inexpressible wound whose immediate consequence is the dislocation, if not transvaluation, of our customary perceptions and feelings and attachments to life. The loss of someone we love creates, in Jacques Lacan's phrase, "a hole in the real,"[6] and it is no accident that this speech sets in motion Hamlet's preoccupation with seeming and being, including the train of images of acting that is crystallized in the play within the play. The peculiar centripetal pull of anger and sorrow that the speech depicts remains as the central undercurrent of that preoccupation, most notably in Hamlet's later soliloquy about the player's imitation of Hecuba's grief:

> Is it not monstrous that this player here,
> But in a fiction, in a dream of passion,
> Could force his soul so to his own conceit
> That from her working all his visage wanned,
> Tears in his eyes, distraction in 's aspect,
> A broken voice, and his whole function suiting
> With forms to his conceit? And all for nothing.
> For Hecuba!
> What's Hecuba to him, or he to Hecuba,
> That he should weep for her? What would he do
> Had he the motive and the cue for passion
> That I have?   (2.2.552–63)

Hamlet then goes on to rebuke himself for his own inaction, but the player's imitation of grief nonetheless moves him internally, as nothing else can, in fact to take action, as he conceives of the idea of staging a play to test both the ghost and the conscience of the King.

After Hamlet finishes answering his mother in the earlier court scene, the King offers his own consolation for Hamlet's grief:

'Tis sweet and commendable in your nature, Hamlet,
To give these mourning duties to your father;
But you must know your father lost a father;
That father lost, lost his; and the survivor bound
In filial obligation for some term
To do obsequious sorrow. But to persever
In obstinate condolement is a course
Of impious stubbornness, 'tis unmanly grief,
It shows a will most incorrect to heaven,
A heart unfortified, a mind impatient,
An understanding simple and unschooled;
For what we know must be, and is as common
As any the most vulgar thing to sense,
Why should we in our peevish opposition
Take it to heart? Fie, 'tis a fault to heaven,
A fault against the dead, a fault to nature,
To reason most absurd, whose common theme
Is death of fathers, and who still hath cried
From the first corpse till he that died today,
"This must be so."   (1.2.97–106)

There is in fact much in this consolation of philosophy which is spiritually sound, and to which every human being must eventually accommodate himself, but it comes at the wrong time, from the wrong person, and in its essential belittlement of the heartache of grief, it comes with the wrong inflection. It is a dispiriting irony of scholarship on this play that so many critics should essentially take such words, from such a king, as a text for their own indictments of Hamlet behavior. What a person who is grieving needs, of course, is not the consolation of words, even words that are true, but sympathy—and this Hamlet does not receive, not from the court, not from his uncle, and more important, not from his own mother, to whom his grief over his father's death is alien and unwelcome.

Notes

1. Cited in Alan S. Downer, *The British Drama* (New York: Appleton-Century-Crofts, 1950), p. 78.

2. I assume throughout this argument that Shakespeare essentially accepts and draws nourishment from the conventions of the revenge drama and that the ghost represents Hamlet's tragic predicament more than he does a strictly moral issue. Shakespeare clearly sophisticates Kyd's conception by conflating the ghost of Andrea and the figure of Revenge and by bringing the ghost directly into the world of the play and into Hamlet's consciousness, but there is little question, either by Hamlet or by us, that Hamlet must eventually obey the ghost's injuction to take revenge. In later dramas like *The Atheist's Tragedy* and *The Revenge of Bussy D'Ambois*, the ghosts themselves remind the heroes that revenge belongs to God, but it is hardly an accident that those plays are neither tragic nor particularly compelling. The whole issue of the ethos of revenge in *Hamlet* is discussed most convincingly, it seems to me, by Helen Gardner in *The Business of Criticism* (Oxford: Oxford Univ. Press, 1959), pp. 35–51, and Roland M. Frye, *The Renaissance Hamlet* (Princeton: Princeton Univ. Press, 1984). For a contrary interpretation of the issue, see especially Fredson Bowers, *Elizabethan Revenge Tragedy* (Princeton: Princton Univ. Press, 1940), and "Hamlet as Minister and Scourge," *PMLA* 70 (1955): 740–49; and Eleanor Prosser, *Hamlet and Revenge* (Stanford: Stanford Univ. Press, 1967).

3. *The Jew of Malta*, ed. N.W. Bawcutt, *The Revels Plays* (Manchester: Manchester Univ. Press, 1978), 3.2.13–14.

4. *The Spanish Tragedy*, ed. Philip Edwards, The Revels Plays (Cambridge: Harvard Univ. Press, 1959).

5. T.S. Eliot, *Selected Essays* (London: Faber and Faber, 1951), p. 145.

6. Jacques Lacan, "Desire and the Interpretation of Desire in Hamlet," *Yale French Studies* 55/56 (1977): 37–39.

MEREDITH ANNE SKURA ON HAMLET'S THEATRICAL SELF-CONSCIOUSNESS

The lord who had directed the prominent players in *Shrew*, *Love's Labour's Lost*, and *Dream* moves to the center of the metadramatic plays in the figures of Hamlet, Duke Vincentio in *Measure for Measure*, and Prospero in *The Tempest*. And with his repositioning, the problematics of theater are combined with questions about government as well as about selfhood. In *Hamlet*, for example, probably the most theatrically self-conscious of all the plays, the arrival of the players at Elsinore recalls the similar arrival in *Shrew*, and Hamlet's greeting recalls the *Shrew* Lord's delighted response to his players. Both men know and welcome the players, and each makes his authority clear by demanding that the players treat with respect an audience who does not really deserve it—Sly in *Shrew* and Polonius in *Hamlet*. Each lectures the players about their own jobs, as if a better judge than they of such things. But in the earlier play the focus was on Sly, as much an actor as the players, and it is Sly's transformation that is mirrored in the inner play when Petruchio transforms Kate from shrew to perfect wife. In the latter the focus is on Hamlet, who is not only an actor but also mast of ceremonies, playwright and prince; it is his story that is mirrored in the inner play, "The Murder of Gonzago." And Hamlet's story, of course, is Denmark's story. Hamlet's refusal of the deceptive roles he finds himself forced to play is part of his recoil from all seeming in a world where hypocrisy taints even love and friendship, and where all human achievement is illusory.[75] His theatrical self-consciousness corresponds to our sense of Denmark as *theatrum mundi*, where "there's a divinity that shapes our ends, / Rough-hew them how we will" (5.2.10–11). Amidst *Hamlet's* encompassing theatricality, a professional actor's psychological concerns, like his financial concerns now that the boy actors are competing in the capital, remain tangential. We need no actor come from the stage to tell us what every sensitive adult should feel in this Denmark.

But just as an actor has private stakes in the play he serves, Hamlet has his own reasons for his obsession with Denmark's playing. Just as the theater serves an actor, the *theatrum mundi* metaphor, as true as Shakespeare has made it here, serves Hamlet; and theater itself provides a way out of his melancholic paralysis. When the Lord in Shew turned from contemplating the image of "grim death" in Sly's drunkenness, to thinking about staging his own play the conjunction seemed accidental. For Hamlet the movement from thoughts to death to "The Murder of Gonzago" seems inevitable in a play where the play-within-a-play marks a turning point for the entire action; but it nonetheless reveals something about him as well as about

Denmark. The players deflect Hamlet from suicide, and they allow him to take control over the situation which has made him powerless.[76] In "The Murder of Gonzago" Hamlet brings his dead father to life again; more importantly, the play gives life to Hamlet's own dead father to life again; more importantly, the play gives life to Hamlet's own dead emotions. Simply by revealing the truth, the play serves as the act of aggression Hamlet could not bring himself otherwise to perform.[77] But in his roles as the play's presenter or chorus and interpreter, Hamlet also changes the revelation into a threat, the history into a prediction. Hamlet makes "Gonazago's" murderer Lucianus into the "nephew to the King," and he cues the actor playing Lucianus with, "the croaking raven doth bellow for revenge" (*Ham.* 3.2.239, 248). But Lucianus is about to commit regicide not revenge—it's Hamlet who is thinking of revenge.[78] Hamlet's passionate involvement in the play emerges in his frenzied remarks to Ophelia ("Lady, shall I lie in your lap?", *Ham.* 3.2.110–11), as well as to Claudius, alternating like Richard III between a "lady's lap" (3H6 3.2.148) and the crown.[79]

In particular, Hamlet becomes as emotionally involved with his audience as any actor does. The performance becomes a hunt, and Claudius the wounded deer. Hamlet's manic crow of delight after Claudius leaves makes the analogy: "Why, let the stricken deer go weep, / The hart ungalled play; / For some must watch while some must sleep, / Thus runs the world away" (*Ham.* 3.2.265–68). The tables have been turned since the *Shrew* Lord found Sly while hunting, and Ford held Falstaff at bay to dis-horn him. Now Hamlet is the hunter who stalks deer with the players, and he boasts to Horatio that his hit in "Gonzago" would earn him "a fellowship in a *cry* of players" (3.2.271–72)—a cry being a canine hunting pack, so-called after the yelping of dogs on a scent.[80] For the moment at least, Hamlet sees the actors as dogs, or as "the 'hounds' in a skimmington-like 'stag-hunt"—like the one in *Wives* that made Falstaff its object "of which the object is to flush and publically pursue an offender against sexual morals."[81] He has gotten into the spirit of the playing he had once disdained. By the end of the play Hamlet has accepted his actor status not only as a willing "seemer," but also as one who depends on the dangerously venal vicissitudes of performance before an audience. "You that look pale and tremble at this chance, / That are but mutes or audience to this act" (*Ham*. 5.2.339–40). The man whose first words had rejected all seeming for "that within which passeth show," dies concerned about how he seems to others: "O God, Horatio, what a wounded name, / Things standing thus unknown, shall I leave behind me" (*Ham*. 5.2.349–50). Appropriately enough when Fortinbras arrives to take over he first likens the death scene to a hung ("This quarry cries on havoc"; Ham. 5.2.375); he ends by making Hamlet into a triumphant actor ("Bear Hamlet like a soldier to the stage"; *Ham*. 5.2.401.)

Notes

75. Like the heroes of the early histories—or the would-be warriors in *Love's Labour's Lost*—Hamlet is called to play an impossibly heroic roles: as "worthy," bequeathed to him by his mythic father; as the morality–play scourge of God (Howard Felperin, *Shakespeare as Representation: Mimesis and Modernity in Elizabethan Tragedy* [Princeton: Princeton University Press, 1977], 44–67); as the revenge play revenger (Mark Rose, *"Hamlet* and the Shape of Revenge," *English Literary Renaissance* [1971]: 132–43); or any number of other roles including, simply, "hypocrite." But unlike Navarre, Hamlet puts those roles in perspective. He is not so much an actor as an actor-manqué, overwhelmed by his sense of the futility of action in the larger theater of the world.

76. In the Quarto they almost literally save him from suicide, arriving as they do after his "to be or not to be" soliloquy. In the Folio, Hamlet does not think about self-slaughter until after his first encounter with the players, but such thoughts disappear when he briefs the players for their court performance. On the timing of the players' arrival see Leo Salingar, "The Players in *Hamlet*," *The Aligarh Journal of English Studies* 6 (1981): 168–93, esp. 170–71.

77. Francis Fergusson, *The Idea of a Theatre* (Garden City: Doubleday, 1953), 135; Barber and Wheeler, *Whole Journey*, 264.

78. David Mann. *The Elizabethan Player: Contemporary Stage Representation*. London: Routledge (1991): 51.

79. See Chapter 3.

80. Before the play when Hamlet explained his plan to Horatio, he had already likened Claudius to his prey: "Observe my uncle. If his occulted guilt / Do not itself unkennel in one speech / It is a damned ghost that we have seen" (*Ham.* 3.2.85–87). Just after the play he suspects that Claudius has sent his agents Rosencrantz and Guildenstern to hunt Hamlet: "Why do you go about to recover the wind of me, as if you would drive me into a toil [net as used in deer hunting]?" (*Ham.* 3.2.37–38).

81. Greene, "Hamlet's Skimmington," 8.

JOHN LEE ON HAMLET'S
SELF-CONSTITUTING SELFHOOD

Shakespeare's Prince Hamlet has a self which is both a part of, and important to, his sense of identity. The last chapter put forward two complementary ways of describing and following this self. 'That Within' the Prince was seen to be an area discrete, though not separate, from his society, and that discreteness was seen to have been self-created; the Prince was seen to possess a self-constituting, as opposed to a self-fashioning, agency. Such an argument refutes the basic thrusts of the arguments of Cultural Materialists and New Historicists concerning English Renaissance literary subjectivity. It also concentrates on the similarities between the Prince's sense of self and more modern senses of self. However, at the heart of the descriptive approaches to self put forward in Chapter 6 is an insistence on the non-essentialist nature of self; Prince Hamlet's senses of self must be historically sited, distinct in various ways from our contemporary sense of self. Prince Hamlet must have aspects of his sense of self that make him of his time; to a point, he must acknowledge Claudius' claim of kinship in this, as in familial matters—no matter how distasteful that kinship may be to him. This chapter focuses on one aspect of his kinship, and so on one difference between the senses of self within *Hamlet* and modern senses of self.

The meaning of 'rhetorical,' as used above, may need explanation. 'Rhetoric' is used here in the sense broached by *in the Sixteenth Century Excluding Drama*: 'Rhetoric', Lewis noted, 'is the greatest barrier between us and our ancestors.'[1] This a rather grand statement, according 'rhetoric' a great and wide-ranging importance in all aspects of culture. Lewis leaves this assertion of importance rather unsubstantiated. One the one hand, he gives as example the sixteenth century's (to his mind) deplorable enjoyment of rhetorical figures for their own sake, and on the other he speaks (very positively) of a different, rhetorical, way of thinking, evidence by the sixteenth century's ability to talk about the humdrum and the profound in the same breath. Each example is given badly, as might be expected to the introduction to a literary guide.

Lewis's use of 'rhetoric' has the virtue of making immediately plan what 'rhetoric' does not mean; 'rhetoric', as Lewis used it and it is here used, does not have its currently dominant sense of an ornamental patterning added to language, which is often seen as marking out that language as deceptive and specious.[2] Rhetoric is something far larger, far more important, and far more positive than that. What that was in the English Renaissance[3] has been the subject of a large body of critical work, carried out over the last forty-five years, and on which the following discussion relies. Central to nearly all of this work is the recognition that 'rhetoric' is not a simple or single activity, but a system. What follows is an outline of the manner in which that recognition came about, and the critical implications of that recognition. (...)

In Chapter 6, metaphor was argued to offer an expressive resource for a person's sense of self, even a self which lacked a modern vocabulary of interiority. It would seem likely that a rhetorical sense of self would express and explore itself through the same complex of imagery which is used to express and explore the nature of rhetoric. If this is so, one might expect to find images of a person's self, within Shakespeare's plays, as images of water. This line of though can be developed through Erasmus' image. If speech is a river, what then is the speaker? Some form of reservoir whose interior is also made up of the same water that composes its world. Such a liquid sense of self might strike us as unlikely; but then one might expect to find particularly unfamiliar a sense of self different from our own. (...)

Such fluidity of form is suggestive of the figure of Proteus, who might be called the Shakespearian god, in the light of literary critics use of Proteus to attempt to define Shakespeare's ability to create character (seen in Part II). Proteus, as has been noted, achieved especial prominence during the Renaissance: in classical myth, Proteus had been a minor sea-god who served Poseidon and had, according to Homer, both the power to change his shape and a vast knowledge; in the Renaissance, Proteus gained in importance as he came to be seen as a symbol of a defining aspect of man's nature. This aspect of Proteus was formulated strikingly by Juan Luis Vives in his *Fabula de homine* (after 1518), which draws on Giovanni Pico della Mirandola's more influential and innovative *De dignitate hominis* (written 1486). In Vives's fable, the world is created as a theatre and play for the gods, and by Jupiter as an after-dinner surprise for the guests at Juno's birthday party. The gods, when they have finished eating, take their seats for the performance, and soon begin discussing who is the best actor on the planet before them. Soon it becomes clear that man deserves the title; he acts different parts with each of his entrances. He can live as insensibly as a plant; or as cunningly as the fox, or as lustfully as a sow; or he can live justly and prudently with others, in the society of a city. (...)

In Montaigne's *Essays* there is a horizontal multiplicity of expression, a variation which, though it spurs and shapes the formal expression of the Essays, can become fatiguing and wearisome. Shakespeare exploits this more negative tradition of interpretation of Protean identity more dramatically. The terror that lies within Pico's 'indeterminate nature' is staged; dramatic persons struggle constantly to be determinate, and occasionally fail, losing hold on their fluid selves, flowing into the invisibility of indeterminacy.

Shakespeare's Prince Hamlet draws on this Protean,

rhetorical sense of self. Hamlet begins, one might say, where Faustus left off. The opening lines of his first soliloquy are a wish for dissolution (here of the flesh) as a means to escape his present predicament: 'Oh that this too too solid Flesh, would melt, / Thaw, and resolue it selfe into a Dew' (I.2.129–30). Hamlet desires the watery nature of a rhetorical self which the solidity of his flesh denies him. His predicament is less pressing than Faustus's; no bell is immediately to sound twelve, and no devils wait to drag the Prince down to hell—though a ghost (after the bell has sounded twelve unheard) will soon come to him, and make the Prince wonder whether he is being tempted to his own damnation. This sense of his over-solid nature is paralleled by Hamlet's sense of a lack of words; the soliloquy which begins with the desire to melt ends with his recognition that, because of the situation he finds himself in, he cannot say what he would wish to do, but must keep his words contained: 'But break my heart, for I must hold my tongue' (I.2.159).

Notes

1. C.S. Lewis, *English Literature in the Sixteenth Century Excluding Drama* (Oxford: Clarendon Press, 1954), 61.

2. Such a negative sense was also current during the English Renaissance, and became more pronounced at the end of the 16th c., with the rise of satire and the plain anti-courtly style, now particularly associated with John Donne. So, to choose an example at random, the Princess Agripyne, in Thomas Dekker's *Old Fortunatus*, can talk of a soldier's wooing as 'home-spun stuff' because 'there's no outlandish thread in it, no rhetoric. A soldier casts no figures to get his mistress' heart.' (In *Thomas Dekker*, ed. Ernest Rhys (London: Vizetelly & Co., 1887), 3.I, p. 339.) However, in Dekker, as in Shakespeare, the use of a copious style of rhetoric does not in general mark the speaker out as untrustworthy, as it begins to do in the plays of Ben Johnson and others. For a discussion of this see Neil Rhodes, *The Power of Eloquence and English Renaissance Literature* (Hemel Hempstead: Harvester Wheatsheaf, 1992).

3. For an account of the relationship between Renaissance, medieval and classical rhetorics, see Kristeller, *Renaissance Thought*, esp. ch. 5.

ROBERT WEIMANN ON ENGLISH PROTESTANTISM AND THE ELIZABETHAN STAGE

As the Elizabethan settlement in politics and religion was drawing to a close, the already existing "religious, social, and cultural lines of cleavage grew sharper than they had been" (Bush, *English Literature* 14). This is not to deny that, politically, a good deal of the Jacobean period continued to enjoy, in Christopher Hill's words, "years of a considerable degree of national unity" (*Collected Essays* 1:4). However, in the field of cultural practices the continuity of a nationally significant inclusiveness was being undermined by, among other things, newly articulate divisions and differentiations, in which the theatre, including relations of writing and playing, figured fairly conspicuously.

The climate of inclusive cultural expectations, in particular what more than a generation ago used to be called "the unity of taste" in the Elizabethan theatre (Harbage, *Shakespeare's Audience* 144),[13] was gradually giving way. In early modern England, the exceptional strength of the "mingle-mangle," that is, the hodge-podge force in what Cornelius Castoriadis defined as the "ensemblist-ensemblizing dimension" of both "social doing" and "social representing/saying" (238) was beginning to exhaust itself.[14] With the first immediate threat of Spanish invasion over, the execution of Essex must have made it difficult to find a consistently strong patriotic focus for an "Elizabethan writing of England" that I, in Richard Helgerson's revealing phrase, could plausibly claim some viable core of interest and resolution among socially and educationally diverse positions.[15] The Elizabethan cultural "ensemble" had in its imaginary institution been witness (again, in Castoriadis' words) to important elements of a self-identical unity of differences"; the days of the cultural alliance approaching an end, the entire "schemata of separation and union" (which mutually implied and presupposed one another) were nearing a state of decomposition" (Castoriadis, *Imaginary Institution* 224). Now the alliance of court, city, and country, so crucial to the formative years of Elizabethan drama, was becoming a thing of the past; henceforth, this alliance could only be sued to evoke nostalgic memories of the days of good queen Bess, as spelled out in the mingle-mangle title of Tarlton's posthumous collection of *His Court Witty Jests, His Sound City Jests, His Country Pretty Jests*, published in 1611. Even before Shakespeare returned to settle in Stratford, theatrical attendance in the London playhouses had reached its peak and was leveling off (Harbage, *Shakespeare's Audience* 38).

The emergence of a vociferous Protestantism in manners and moral coincided, by 1580 or thereabout, with a final and irretrievable rejection of the stage as a Protestant medium. Together, these trends pointed to the exclusion of the licentious and the withdrawal of the worthy from important cultural practices. As English Protestantism spread at the grass roots, as the channels of education broadened, the technology of print expanded, and reading and writing were more widely practiced, cultural and political articulation and discussion reached a level unprecedented in its dimensions.[16] Sir Robert Cecil in 1601 was perplexed that "parliament-matters are ordinarily talked of in the streets."[17] It was in this context that, I suggest, the call for soci-cultural reform and refinement reflected an ambivalent set of fervid hopes and deep anxieties. This was the time when, with hindsight one may perhaps say, it was high time that a sharper line was drawn between polite and popular pursuits, between "judicious" and vulgar standards in cultural production and consumption.

For the theatre, this moment was one of a particular dynamic. If my reading in the preceding section is not wide of the mark, the end of the alliance between drama and Protestantism or, as Paul White calls it, "the break-up of the pro-drama consensus among Protestants" (164), while it certainly reduced the range of patronage, was not of course the end of itinerant playing. On the contrary, as the *REED* records suggest, this period was preceded, in Bradbrook's phrase, by a "multiplication of troupes of poor players in the late sixties and early seventies" (*Rise of the Common Player* 125). Now the scene was set for a recrudescence of the most variegated secular performance practices. The end of Protestant inspiration and patronage coincided with the beginning of a withdrawal from the theatre of the better and, even, the middling sort, leading to the demand to "reform" the profession (the verb is used twice in *Hamlet* 3.2.36; 38). But these demands came at a time when, paradoxically, both playwrights and performers continued to straddle the emerging cultural divisions. Here I do not wish to anticipate a reading of the complex constellation in which *Hamlet* finds itself between a persistent element of inclusiveness and the assertion of a new authority of the "judicious." Let me content myself with the observation that, at the turn of the century, Shakespeare's plays thrived in a set of circumstances in which it appeared not only possible but, in view of continued audience appeal and attendance, desirable to confront and, even, playfully use elements of both "separation" and "union" in a multiple constellation of theatrical discourses and practices.

In order to illustrate the paradox involved in these circumstances, it must suffice here to note that, on the one hand, Shakespeare's plays continued to draw on a fairly inclusive frame of reference. The same Hamlet, who enjoins "modesty" and "discretion" upon the players (words that, as we shall presently see, are central concepts in the language of reform) is perfectly prepared to tolerate, even to exploit, the absence of such discretion in his encounter with the grave-digger.

> By the Lord, Horatio, this three years I have took note
> of it: the age is grown so pick'd that the toe of the peasant
> comes so near the heel of the courtier, he galls his kibe.
> (5.1.138–41)

At this point, there prevails some sort of balance between "union" and "separation," inclusiveness and stratification. It is an observation that neatly marks both the "mingle-mangle" of mobility and the awareness of social difference, with an implied need, or so it seems, for imminent differentiation of social status. The Prince of Denmark seizes on a new sense of both social collision *and* cultural proximity inside and outside the theatre. But hen he does so without himself proceeding to any gesture of exclusion. Inspired as well as perhaps appalled by the mother-wit of a "peasant," the Prince resolves to "speak by the card," accepting the clownish mode of quibbling contrariety as a challenge ("or equivocation will undo us" 13*) in his own freely initiated communication with the grave-digger.

However, Shakespeare's equivocal position—the demand for "reform" and the refusal to comply with it in one and the same play—is largely unparalleled. Elsewhere in the Elizabethan theatre, the forces of differentiation and exclusion were emphatically gaining in strength. At the turn of the century, even before *Hamlet*, as we know the play, was first produced, certain performance practices were increasingly singled out as a target for attack.

Notes

13. See also Sisson, *Le Goût public et le théâtre élisabéthain jusqu'à la mort de Shakespeare*, esp. 35–51.

14. I have read and documented the Tudor socio-cultural mingle-mangle at length in my dissertation (Humboldt University, 1955) *Drama und Wirklichkeit in der Shakespearezeit* 13–180, and more briefly in *Shakespeare and the Popular Tradition in the Theater*, especially the chapters "Toward the Culture of a Nation" and "Sociology of the Elizabethan Stage" 161–77. In more recent social and political historiography, among studies addressing the political, social and cultural relations behind the Elizabethan Settlement, I have found particularly helpful, in addition to what has been already cited: Elton, *Policy and Police*; Hurstfield, *Freedom, Corruption and Government in Elizabethan England*; MacCaffrey, *The Shaping of the Elizabethan Regime*; Hassell Smith, *Gentry and Court*; James, *Family Lineage, and Civil Society*; Collinson, *The Elizabethan Puritan Movement*; Wrightson, *English Society, 1580–1680*.

15. Helgerson, in Forms of Nationhood, proceeds to view Shakespeare's position in the theatre as more or less marked by a strategy of "exclusion."

16. The most persuasive assemblage of evidence is still Ferguson's *The Articulate Citizen and the English Renaissance*.

17. Cit. by Hill, "The Pre-Revolutionary Decades," *The Collected Essays* 1:10.

In one way *Hamlet* was not a new departure for a poet capable of radically transforming existing dramas. In this case, he was able to draw on a work that was presumably not his own but which the Chamberlain's men performed, or the now-missing *Hamlet*—a revenge play with a ghost—which his colleagues had staged at Burbage's Theater before it apparently went briefly to Newington. It may have been by Kyd, but, again, its author is unknown. It was a noisy if not a tumultuous and ungainly work, conjured up in an allusion in Lodge's *Wit's Misery* (1596) to one who 'looks as pale as the Visard of the ghost which cried so miserably at the Theator like an oister wife, Hamlet, revenge'.[5] Shakespeare had at least one other ready-made play in mind. In Kyd's *The Spanish Tragedy*, he found a kind of kitchen cupboard full of 'revenge' motifs and devices, which must have gathered interest for him after he had discovered in Belleforest's *Histoires tragiques* (1570), the revamped tale of a lively avenger, Amleth, who had earlier appeared in Saxo's twelfth-century *Historiae Danicae*.

Also, his new play relates to the theatrical present. *Hamlet* responds to a mood, noticeable by 1599, entailing the charge that the 'public' stages are crowd-pleasing, unintelligent and lacking in audacity. The tragedy's complex and intelligent hero, its fresh and subtle word-play, brilliantly evoked setting and new treatment of the revenge motif, refined and elegant soliloquies, and philosophical richness all advertise the sophistication of the Globe's public stage. The play has humour to match the satire of new 'wits', and no trace of insular narrowness. The hero is a scholar of Wittenberg—the university of Luther and Faustus—and the action involves not only Denmark and Germany, but Norway, France, England, Poland, even a king's 'Switzers' and (in its atmosphere of intrigue and lechery) a popular notion of Italy. Yet this tragedy is far more than an advertisement for the Globe or a response to a commercial situation.

With its wealth of meanings, ambiguities, high-handed contradictions and supreme and troubling beauty, *Hamlet* is nearly a chaos. It takes enormous risks as a work for the popular theatre and an easily baffled public. *Julius Caesar*—by comparison—is neatly well-mannered, almost timid, and lacking anything like this work's exuberance. The confident writing in *Hamlet* suggests a poet whose best insights and observations are all before him. Suddenly, his whole experience of life is relevant, or the Muses have made it so: indeed Hamlet is often felt to be an all-accommodating, 'personal' expression of its author, and editors point to a few oddities. The Folio and Second Quarto texts together show that Shakespeare wrote too many lines for the work, or enough to keep actors on stage for four or five hours. If the Second Quarto is based on his 'foul papers' (or working MS) as editors believe, the MS may have been a mess of inserts, cross-outs, and badly aligned or missing speech-headings. A compositor in setting the Second Quarto resorted to the inferior but printed First Quarto to make sense of what he saw.

Still, *Hamlet* was meticulously planned. Its ease of style disguises the real intensity of the author's intellectual effort. His sonnet-writing offered one answer, at least, to what has been called the most taxing problem in writing a revenge tragedy, or how to fill in the long interval between the commission of the crime which calls for vengeance, and the carrying out of revenge in Act V. In some sonnets, Shakespeare explores paradoxes almost too refined for the stage, as when he puts morality to the test in Sonnet 121. Is it better to act brutishly, or only to be thought vile by others? ''Tis better to be vile than vile esteemed', he begins in a densely complex lyric, which stands morality on its head. *Hamlet*'s revenge framework gives scope to a hero of sonnet-like nuances of thought and self-awareness, or to a Renaissance man with a 'courtier's, soldier's, scholar's eye, tongue, sword', in Ophelia's view, who is disposed to fully contemplated action.[6] The effect, however, is to displace the revenge theme itself with emphasis on the hero, the Danish court, and issues of power politics.

But if *Hamlet* is activated by a political power-struggle, this is not what sets the work apart. Critics have drawn attention not only to the work's political nature but to how 'interchangeably diversified', as Dr Johnson once put it, the scenes are in content and feeling. 'It would be hard to think of anything less like a classical tragedy', writes one of *Hamlet*'s modern editors, G. R. Hibbard. 'In it the Elizabethan tendency to all-inclusiveness is pushed to the limit by a playwright who is fully conscious that he is doing just that.' One topic impinges upon another, and yet there is a fertile duality in the organized treatment of Elsinore, and that is what most consistently distinguishes Shakespeare's attitude to a Danish milieu. He may not have travelled in Denmark, but his fellow actors Will Kempe, George Bryan, and Thomas Pope had acted in 1585 and 1586 at Elsinore or the Danish Helsingør (which is the name of a township and not of a castle). The medieval castle of Krogen, a damp and ruinous fortress, had then been transformed into the Renaissance palace of Kronborg, full of costly furnishings and graced with colour and light: its renewal was being celebrated.[7] The English actors saw King Frederik II's new, affluent Denmark on the very wave of its emergence from medieval constraints. Denmark's cultural atmosphere, then, was unique, memorable, and not unrelated to the course of English history and Shakespeare's life in the Jacobean age ahead. It was Frederik's daughter Anna who married Scotland's James VI, and, as his consort, later became England's Queen. Her brother King Christian IV did even more than his father to modernize Danish society with an army of builders and painters. At Helsingør, Shakespeare's actors had seen a distinctive example of the northern Renaissance.

Notes

5. Sig. H4.

6. *Hamlet*, III. i. 154; cf. *Hamlet*, ed. Hibbard, 32.

7. *Hamlet*, ed. Hibbard, 29; Barbara Everett, *Young Hamlet: Essays: on Shakespeare's Tragedies* (Oxford, 1989), 3–8.

Works by William Shakespeare*

Henry VI, part 1, circa 1589–1592.

Henry VI, part 2, circa 1590–1592.

Henry VI, part 3, circa 1590–1592.

Richard III, circa 1591–1592.

The Comedy of Errors, circa 1592–1594.

Titus Andronicus, 1594.

The Taming of the Shrew, 1594.

The Two Gentlemen of Verona, 1594.

Love's Labor's Lost, circa 1594–1595.

Sir Thomas More, circa 1594–1595.

King John, circa 1594–1596.

Richard II, circa 1595.

Romeo and Juliet, circa 1595–1596.

A Midsummer Night's Dream, circa 1595–1596.

The Merchant of Venice, circa 1596–1597.

Henry IV, part 1, circa 1596–1597.

Henry IV, part 2, circa 1597.

The Merry Wives of Windsor, 1597.

Much Ado About Nothing, circa 1598–99.

Henry V, 1599.

Julius Caesar, 1599.

As You Like It, circa 1599–1600.

Hamlet, circa 1600–1601.

Twelfth Night, circa 1601–1602.

Troilus and Cressida, 1601–02.

All's Well That Ends Well, 1602–1603.

Measure for Measure, 1604.

Othello, 1604.

King Lear, 1606.

Timon of Athens, 1605–1608.

Macbeth, 1606.

Anthony and Cleopatra, 1606–1607.

Pericles, circa 1607–1608.

Coriolanus, circa 1607–1608.

Cymbeline, 1609.

The Winter's Tale, 1611.

The Tempest, 1611.

Cardenio, circa 1612–1613.

Henry VIII, 1613.

The Two Noble Kinsmen, 1613.

*Dates by production

Annotated Bibliography

Alexander, Peter. *Hamlet: Father and Son*. Oxford: The Clarendon Press, 1953.

The text of a lecture delivered at University College, Alexander begins his discussion of older Shakespearean actors, such as David Garrick, and their audiences' expectations, through modern day adaptations such as Sir Laurence Olivier's interpretation of Prince Hamlet. Alexander stresses the need for a careful examination of the critical tradition of such renowned critics as Harley Granville-Barker and A.C. Bradley and the validity of applying terms from Greek tragedy, such as *hamartia* and *catharsis*, to Shakespearean tragedy.

Bloom, Harold. Hamlet: *Poem Unlimited*. New York: Riverhead Books, 2003.

A postlude to Harold Bloom's previous essay on *Hamlet* in *Shakespeare and the Invention of the Human*, this short book evaluates the critical issue of theatricality in both the character of Hamlet and the play. Hamlet is discussed as both a consummate actor and playwright, a changeling who has fathered himself, and a master at manipulating others.

———. *Shakespeare and the Invention of the Human*. New York: Riverhead Books, 1998.

Harold Bloom focuses on the various sources for *Hamlet*, and is of the opinion that the *Ur-Hamlet* was written by Shakespeare, sometime between 1588–1589. He discusses Hamlet as a charismatic, a character without a rival and, thus, one who defies definition. "There is no 'real' Hamlet as there is no 'real' Shakespeare: the character, like the writer, is a reflecting pool, a spacious mirror in which we needs must see ourselves."

Bradley, A.C. *Shakespearean Tragedy*, Second Edition. London: Macmillan and Co., 1905.

A compilation of lectures by Shakespearean scholar A.C. Bradley discuss the substance and construction of Shakespearean tragedy, as well the major tragedies *Hamlet, Othello, King Lear*, and *Macbeth*.

Cavell, Stanley. "Hamlet's Burden of Proof." *Disowning Knowledge*. Cambridge and New York: Cambridge University Press, 1987: 179–91.

A discussion of Hamlet's character as possessing an extreme perception of theatre as an inescapable symbol of the human condition. And that consciousness is at odds with his eternal refusal to become a part of mankind. Cavell maintains that Hamlet can only overcome that refusal at the point of his own death.

Charney, Maurice. *Hamlet's Fictions*. New York and London: Routledge, 1988.

Focuses on *Hamlet* as a work of theatrical imagination, a play of speculation and displacement. For Charney, the critical problem is how to reconcile modern discourse within the context of the language and theatrical context of the original play that Shakespeare wrote and presented around the beginning of the seventeenth century.

Everett, Barbara. *Young Hamlet: Essays on Shakespeare's Tragedies*. Oxford: Clarendon Press and New York: Oxford University Press, 1989.

Discusses *Hamlet* as a work of "the most formally inventive of all literary geniuses" and its representation of ordinary human experience. In discussing Hamlet's modernity, Everett presents a comprehensive range of literary works and accounts for its reception within a historical context.

Forker, Charles R. *Fancy's Images: Contexts, Settings, and Perspectives in Shakespeare and His Contemporaries*. Carbondale: Southern Illinois University Press, 1990.

Divided into three main sections, Forker discusses theatrical self-consciousness; the pastoral tradition and its importance for the Elizabethan stage; and familial issues. All three sections discuss *Hamlet* at length.

Goddard, Harold C. *The Meaning of Shakespeare*. Chicago: The University of Chicago Press, 1951.

Sees Hamlet as the culmination of Shakespeare's greatest characters, for whom there will never exist a theory to fully explain his personality, and the play as possessing a secret that will never yield to disclosure. Goddard sees Hamlet as Shakespeare's reconstituted man, highly individualized, though comprised of the virtues of a multitude of literary predecessors. He concludes by stating that "Hamlet has the creative instinct and capacity to alter the royal occupation from what it has always been, war, to what it ought to be, art."

Greenblatt, Stephen. *Hamlet in Purgatory*. Princeton: Princeton University Press, 2001.

Discusses the significance of Purgatory, "the middle space of the realm of the dead" in texts of the late Middle Ages and the sixteenth and early seventeenth century attack by English Protestants. Greenblatt focuses on Shakespeare's appropriation of the Protestant response in *Hamlet*.

Honan, Park. *Shakespeare: A Life*. Oxford: Oxford University Press, 1998.

This comprehensive volume on Shakespeare's life provides in-depth biographical information and chronicles his development as a playwright against the political and social context of the time.

Honigmann, E.A.J. "Hamlet as Observer and Consciousness." *Shakespeare: Seven Tragedies: The Dramatist's Manipulation of Response*. London and Basingstoke: The Macmillan Press Ltd, 1976: 54–76.

Compares Hamlet to Brutus, both of whom he describes as intellectual heroes, finding the former to be immensely more appealing for, among other things, his sense of humor and all-embracing temperament. Maintains that with

Hamlet, Shakespeare knew he was addressing a different audience—one which had faith in the hero's judgment. Honigmann also believes that *Hamlet* is peopled with "exceptionally watchful secondary characters."

Hubert, Judd D. "Hamlet: Student Prince and Actor." *The Dialectic of Discovery: Essays on the Teaching and Interpretation of Literature Presented to Lawrence E. Harvey.* Edited by John D. Lyons and Nancy J. Vickers. Lexington, Kentucky: *French Forum* (1984):132–44.

Discusses the many instances of intellectuality in *Hamlet*, citing its student characters; its protagonist who prefers knowledge to power; its frequent reliance on books and Hamlet as the perfect scholar possessing an ability to transform his observations into a bookish equivalent. Hubert maintains that in creating the character Hamlet, Shakespeare was rewriting several predecessor texts, including those of Seneca, Cicero, Virgil, and Horace.

Lanham, Richard A. "Superposed Plays." From The *Motives of Eloquence: Literary Rhetoric in the Renaissance.* New Haven: Yale University Press, 1976.

Lanham identifies two parallel plots in Hamlet that work at cross-purposes with each other. The first plot belongs to the hero Laertes and is a conventional revenge tragedy while the second and more compelling plot belongs to Hamlet, the consummate actor and playwright, a very unconventional hero in Shakespeare's counter-revenge play.

Lee, John. *Shakespeare's* Hamlet *and the Controversies of Self.* Oxford and New York: Oxford University Press, 2000.

Examines the question of whether Prince Hamlet has a self-constituting sense of self. Organized in three sections, Lee discusses the contemporary academic debate as well as the critical debate of the seventeenth, eighteenth, and nineteenth centuries. Part III takes up the issue of Hamlet's identity and the problem in describing the interiority of a literary person, which Lee maintains is self-constituting rather than self-fashioning.

Mack, Maynard. "The World of *Hamlet*." *The Yale Review* 41 (1952): 502–23.

Discusses Hamlet's imaginative world as having three basic attributes: the mysteriousness that persists in, among other things, questions about his character and his delay; the problematic nature of reality and its relationship to appearance; and the art of the theatre. Concludes that Hamlet dies with a soldier's honors because he has accepted the world as a duel with evil and demonstrated the courage of "entering into the abyss of himself," a quote borrowed from William Butler Yeats.

———. "The Name of Action." *Killing the King: Three Studies in Shakespeare's Tragic Structure*. New Haven: Yale University Press (1973): 75–137.

Discusses *Hamlet* in terms of Shakespeare's preoccupation with kingship in a culture like that of Queen Elizabeth's where the most popular books included the histories of kings, Machiavelli's works and Spenser's poetry. Maintains that Hamlet, though he does very little in terms of action, imaginatively embodies the entire range of possible experience within his very complex consciousness.

Miola, Robert S. *Shakespeare the Classical Tragedy: The Influence of Seneca*. Oxford and New York: Oxford University Press, 1992.

Discusses Seneca's influence on Shakespeare and focuses on Senecan characters, language, and symbolism, and Seneca's plays themselves. In his chapter, Senecan Revenge," Miola discusses *Hamlet* in terms of Shakespeare's revision of the "monomaniacal revenger" of Senecan drama into a tragic hero who evolves during the course of the drama, a hero able to arouse both pity and terror.

Pirie, David B, ed. *William Empson: Essays on Shakespeare*. Cambridge: Cambridge University Press, 1986.

A collection of the late critic's work includes revised and

updated essays on the ambiguity of Shakespeare's plays, focusing on *Hamlet, Macbeth*, and the character of Falstaff. It also includes an essay on the architecture of The Globe Theater.

Skura, Meredith Anne. "Theater as Reflecting Glass: The Two-way Mirror in *Shakespeare the Actor and the Purposes of Playing*. Chicago and London: The University of Chicago Press, 1993.

Skura explores the important issue of what it meant to be an actor in Shakespeare's England, demonstrating why knowledge of actual theatrical practices is essential for understanding both Shakespeare's plays and the theatricality of everyday life in early modern England. Chapter Six discusses Hamlet's statements about mirrors from the perspective of a sixteenth-century understanding of mirrors functioning as a tool to reveal something unavailable to the unaided eye.

States, Bert O. *HAMLET and the Concept of Character*. Baltimore: The Johns Hopkins University Press, 1992.

Discusses both Hamlet as a literary character created to persuasively support the needs of the plot and *Hamlet* as a play possessing many interesting characterizations. States discusses melancholia as a loss of faith in the world and the other characters comprising "the Hamlet family" who serve as "satellite" figures reflecting on Hamlet's personality and predicament.

Thomson, Peter. "*Hamlet* and the Actor in Shakespeare's Theatre." *Shakespeare's Theatre*. London and Boston: Routledge & Kegan Paul, 1983: 109–35.

Provides a thorough introduction to the historical circumstances of the Globe Theatre and its actors. Discusses Hamlet as a self-conscious play about acting and accounts for many theatrical metaphors and direct references that relate to the Elizabethan theatre.

Weimann, Robert. *Shakespeare and the Popular Tradition in the Theater: Studies in the Social Dimension of Dramatic Form and Function.* Edited by Robert Schwartz. Baltimore: The Johns Hopkins University Press, 1978.

Focuses on the ways in which the theatrical and poetic dimensions interact in Shakespeare's plays within the context of Elizabethan society, theater, and language. Extensive discussion of a wide range of themes in *Hamlet* including a discussion of Hamlet's character as a poetically unified individuality.

Contributors

Harold Bloom is Sterling Professor of the Humanities at Yale University and Henry W. and Albert A. Berg Professor of English at the New York University Graduate School. He is the author of over 20 books, including *Shelley's Mythmaking* (1959), *The Visionary Company* (1961), *Blake's Apocalypse* (1963), *Yeats* (1970), *A Map of Misreading* (1975), *Kabbalah and Criticism* (1975), *Agon: Toward a Theory of Revisionism* (1982), *The American Religion* (1992), *The Western Canon* (1994), and *Omens of Millennium: The Gnosis of Angels, Dreams, and Resurrection* (1996). *The Anxiety of Influence* (1973) sets forth Professor Bloom's provocative theory of the literary relationships between the great writers and their predecessors. His most recent books include *Shakespeare: The Invention of the Human* (1998), a 1998 National Book Award finalist, *How to Read and Why* (2000), *Genius: A Mosaic of One Hundred Exemplary Creative Minds* (2002), and *Hamlet: Poem Unlimited* (2003). In 1999, Professor Bloom received the prestigious American Academy of Arts and Letters Gold Medal for Criticism, and in 2002 he received the Catalonia International Prize.

Janyce Marson is a doctoral student at New York university. She is writing a dissertation on the rhetoric of the mechanical in Wordsworth, Coleridge, and Mary Shelley.

Harley Granville-Barker was a prominent Shakespearean scholar and playwright. He is the author of *Associating with Shakespeare* (1932), *Prefaces to Shakespeare* (1946–1947), *The Exemplary Theatre* (1922), and *The Madras House, A Comedy in Four Acts* (1922).

E.E. Stoll was a prominent Shakespearean scholar. He is the author of *Shakespeare's Young Lovers* (1937); *The Alexander Lectures at the University of Toronto, 1935* (1966), *Shakespeare Studies, Historical and Comparative in Method* (1927), and *From*

Shakespeare to Joyce: Authors and Critics, Literature and Life (1944).

A.C. Bradley was a pre-eminent Shakespearean scholar of the late 18th and early 19th centuries. Bradley held professorships of modern literature at the University of Liverpool, of English language and literature at the University of Glasgow, and of poetry at Oxford University, best known for his book *Shakespearean Tragedy* (1904). Bradley also published *Oxford Lectures on Poetry* (1909), which includes an essay on Shakespeare's *Antony and Cleopatra*, and *A Miscellany* (1929), in which a well-known commentary on Tennyson's *In Memoriam* appears.

William Empson was a pre-eminent English scholar and poet and held professorships at Cambridge University and the University of Sheffield. His *Seven Types of Ambiguity* (1930), a study of the meanings of poetry, is a classic of modern literary criticism. It was followed by *Some Versions of Pastoral* (1935) and *The Structure of Complex Words* (1951). In *Milton's God* (1961), Empson engaged in a vehement attack on Puritanism. His poetry *Poems* (1935), and *The Gathering Storm* (1940) was noted for its wit and metaphysical conceits. A collected edition of his poems appeared in 1955. William Empson was knighted in 1979.

Harold C. Goddard was Professor of English at Swarthmore College and the University of Chicago. He is the author of *Studies in New England Transcendentalism* (1908) and *The Meaning of Shakespeare* (1951).

William Hazlitt was an English essayist and literary critic of the Romantic period. Among his own best works are *Characters of Shakespeare's Plays* (1818), *Lectures on the English Poets* (1818–19) and *The Spirit of the Age* (1825).

A. D. Nuttall is Professor of English at Oxford University. He is the author of several books, including *Openings: Narrative*

Beginnings from the Epic to the Novel (1992), *The Alternative Trinity: Gnostic Heresy in Marlowe, Milton, and Blake* (1998), and *Why Does Tragedy Give Pleasure?* (1996).

Francis Fergusson is the author of *Trope and Allegory: Themes Common to Dante and Shakespeare* (1977), and *Literary Landmarks: Essays on the Theory and Practice of Literature* (1975).

Charles R. Forker is Professor of English Emeritus at Indiana University. He is the author *Skull Beneath the Skin: The Achievement of John Webster* (1986), and editor of *King Richard the Second* (2002) for the Arden Shakespeare series.

Bert O. States is Professor Emeritus of Dramatic Arts at the University of California, Santa Barbara. He is the author of *The Rhetoric of Dreams* (1988), *HAMLET and the Concept of Character* (1992), *The Pleasure of the Play* (1994), and *Seeing in the Dark: Reflections on Dreams and Dreaming* (1997).

John Wilders is Professor Emeritus of the Humanities, Middlebury College, and Emeritus Fellow of Worcester College, University of Oxford. He is the author of *The Lost Garden: A View of Shakespeare's English and Roman History Plays* (1978) and most recently has edited an edition of *Anthony and Cleopatra* for Arden (1995).

Arthur Kirsch is Alice Griffin Professor of English Emeritus at the University of Virginia. He is the author of several books, including *Shakespeare and the Experience of Love* (1981), "Hamlet's Grief" (1981), and editor of *Lectures on Shakespeare/W.H. Auden* (2000).

Meredith Anne Skura is a Professor of English at Rice University. She is the author of *The Literary Use of the Psychoanalytic Process* (1981) and "Discourse and the Individual: The Case of Colonialism in *The Tempest*" (2000).

John Lee is a Lecturer in English at the University of Bristol. He is the author of "The Man Who Mistook his Hat: Stephen Greenblatt and the Anecdote" (1995), and "On Reading *The Tempest* Autobiographically: Ben Jonson and *The New Inn*" (1996).

Robert Weimann is Professor of Drama at the University of California, Irvine and a member of the Berlin-Brandenburg Academy of Arts. He is the author of several books, including *Authority and Representation in Early Modern Discourse* (1996), and Shakespeare *and the Popular Tradition in the Theater: Studies in the Social Dimension of Dramatic Form and Function* (1978).

Park Honan is Professor Emeritus of English at the School of English, University of Leeds. He is the author of several books, including *Authors' Lives: On Literary Biography and the Arts of Language* (1990) and *Jane Austen: Her Life* (1987).

Acknowledgments

"The Nature of the Play" by Harley Granville-Barker. From *Prefaces to Shakespeare: Hamlet*. London: Sidgwick & Jackson, Ltd. (1933): 1–4. © 1933 by Sidgwick & Jackson, Ltd. Reprinted by permission.

"Chapter II: Hamlet's Fault in the Light of Other Tragedies" by E.E. Stoll. From *Hamlet: A Historical and Comparative Study*. Minneapolis: University of Minnesota, 1912: 16–20. © 1912 by the University of Minnesota. Reprinted by permission.

"William Shakespeare: Hamlet" by Harold Bloom. From *How to Read and Why*. New York: Scribner, 2000: 201–205. © 2000 by Harold Bloom. Reprinted by permission.

"Hamlet as the Limit of Stage Drama" by Harold Bloom. From *Hamlet: Poem Unlimited*. New York: Riverhead Books, 2003: 129–133. © 2003 by Harold Bloom. Reprinted by permission.

"Hamlet" by A.C. Bradley. From *Shakespearean Tragedy*, Second Edition by A.C. Bradley. London: Macmillan and Co., 1905: 125–127. © 1905 by Macmillan and Co. Reprinted by permission.

"Hamlet" by William Empson. From William Empson: *Essays on Shakespeare*. Ed. David B. Pirie. Cambridge and New York: Cambridge University Press, 1986: 79–83. © 1986 by William Empson. Reprinted by permission.

"Hamlet" by Harold C. Goddard. From *The Meaning of Shakespeare*. Chicago: The University of Chicago Press: 331–33. © 1951 by The University of Chicago Press. Reprinted by permission.

Press, 1993: 140–42. © 1993 by The University of Chicago Press. Reprinted by permission.

"A King of Infinite Space" by John Lee. From *Shakespeare's* Hamlet *and the Controversies of Self*. Oxford and New York: Oxford University Press, 2000: 209–210; 216; and 221–23. © 2000 by John Lee. Reprinted by permission.

"Histories in Elizabethan Performance" by Robert Weimann. From *Author's Pen and Actor's Voice: Playing and Writing in Shakespeare's Theatre*. Cambridge and New York: Cambridge University Press, 2000: 121–23. © 2000 by Robert Weimann. Reprinted by permission.

"Hamlet's Questions" by Park Honan. From *Shakespeare: A Life*. Oxford and New York: Oxford University Press, 1998: 279–82. © 1998 by Park Honan. Reprinted by permission.

Index

funeral of, 32–3
on Hamlet's disarray, 24
Hamlet's rejection of, 27
madness of, 30
praise of Hamlet by, 73
Orestes (Greek mythology), 61–2
Osric (*Hamlet*), 33, 44–5
Othello (Shakespeare), 12, 71

P

Passionate Pilgrim, The, 12
Plots, two parallel, 15–6
Poets' War (1599–1601), 14–5
Polonius (*Hamlet*), 19
death of, 29–30
on Hamlet's "lunacy," 24–5
as a rhetorician, 16
Protestantism, 88
Proteus (Greek mythology), 85

R

Rape of Lucrece (Shakespeare), 12
Reader. *See* Audience
Relativism, 58–9
Revenge theme, 15
grief and, 74–5
Hamlet's reflections on Claudius
and, 28–9
morality and, 92
popularity of, 74
Shakespeare transforming from
original Hamlet story, 61
Shakespeare's new treatment of,
91
See also Delay and inaction
Rhetoric, 83–5
Richard II (Shakespeare*)*, 35, 64
Romeo and Juliet (Shakespeare), 12
Rosencrantz and Guildenstern
(*Hamlet*), 20
escorting Hamlet to England, 30
execution of, 34
Polonius's corpse and, 29
trying to discover cause of
Hamlet's madness, 25–7

S

Selfhood, 83–6
Setting, modern, 61
Shakespeare, Hamnet (son), 9–10,
11, 12, 52
Shakespeare, Judith (daughter), 11
Shakespeare, Susanna (daughter), 11
Shakespeare, William
alternative vision to religious texts
by, 40
biographical sketch of, 11–3
learning playwright's trade, 35–6
literature of, invention of the
human in, 41
Poets' War and, 14
relationship between Hamlet and,
9–10
works by, 94–5
Skura, Meredith Anne, 79
Soliloquies of Hamlet
on bestial oblivion, 45–6
first, 23, 86
on Hamlet's delay, 30
Hamlet's theatricality and, 26
Spanish Tragedy, The (Kyd), 38, 57,
61, 75, 91
Spurgeon, Caroline, 49–50
States, Bert O., 67
Stoicism, 58
Stoll, E.E., 37
Style, 92–3
Symbolism, theatre, 64–6

T

Taming of the Shrew (Shakespeare),
79–80, 81
Theater
call for reform in, 88–9
Elizabethan, 87–8, 90, 93
rivalry in, 14
Shakespeare's use of language
from, 63–4
symbolism of, 64–6
Theatrical self-consciousness, 79–82
Titus Andronicus (Shakespeare), 12